Energy Security in Nigeria's Gas Sector

Elo Adhekpukoli

ISBN-13: 978-1512004663

Printed by:
CreateSpace
An Amazon.com company

This book is available on Amazon.com and other retail outlets, book stores, online stores, Kindle and other devices.

DEDICATION

I dedicate this book to my parents, John and Anna Adhekpukoli.

CONTENTS

ACKNOWLEDGMENTS

This book is an adaptation of my LLM research thesis at the University of Lagos. I appreciate my supervisor, Dr. Adedayo Ayoade for his valuable advice and suggestions. I also appreciate Mr. Dapo Akinosun, who encouraged me to pursue my interest in energy law at the beginning of my legal career.

PREFACE

Energy resources are indispensable in driving development. Without energy, the world will simply grind to a halt. Gas, as an energy resource has gained the ascendency in recent times and will be increasingly important as a back up and alternative to oil. Nigeria is beginning to shift her attention to gas both as a means of fueling industrial development and as a major revenue earner. Gas is no longer considered as a by-product of crude oil meant for the flare stacks and Nigeria is beginning to realize that. Ending gas flaring in Nigeria is therefore not only an environmental concern anymore but is now of major economic concern. The trend now is towards effective utilization of gas resources. Gas has tremendous potential for Nigeria's socio-economic development. Nigeria needs gas as an alternative cooking fuel for fire wood to check deforestation. The bulk of Nigeria's power generation capacity comes from gas-fired power stations. Nigeria needs gas to power the existing thermal power stations and new power plants otherwise the power revolution will fail. More industries are beginning to use gas as fuel to power their factories. The main driver of gas utilization projects in Nigeria is the Federal Government's desire to create more wealth and diversify the economy of the country.

Nigeria is currently faced with the problem of securing adequate gas production and supply for both domestic and export use. Security in gas supply in Nigeria was and is still plagued by gas flaring, inadequate gas pipeline infrastructure network, uncompetitive domestic gas pricing, absence of standard contractual framework for gas production like the standard Production Sharing Contracts for crude oil, political risks like militancy, vandalism and restiveness. The development of shale gas in the United States and new gas discoveries in Eastern Africa also pose major threats to Nigeria's gas export market share in the long term. Nigeria's energy security in gas would mainly be determined by investments in gas development and such investments would be scarce without a definitive, comprehensive legal regime and good investment climate for gas.

Nigeria's current legal framework is not adequate to ensure energy security in gas. The political will of successive governments to continue with policies of previous regimes have largely determined the extent of developments in the gas sector. The Petroleum Act of 1969 is too oil-centric. Until 2008, when the National Domestic Gas Supply and Price Regulations were made, the major gas-specific legislations were the Associated Gas Re-Injection Act (AGRA), 1979 (as amended) and the Nigeria Liquefied Natural Gas (NLNG) Act, 1989. AGRA was mainly focused on ending gas flaring and was not so much about gas utilization, while the NLNG was focused on tax incentives for the Nigeria Liquefied Natural Gas Limited. The National Domestic Gas Supply and Price Regulations 2008 were aimed at securing gas supply for Nigeria's domestic market and regulating domestic gas price until the market becomes fully developed.

Between 1979 and 2008, the major developments in Nigeria's gas sector were driven by policies. In 2008, a comprehensive policy for gas, the Nigerian Gas Master Plan, was put in place by the Nigerian government. The Nigerian government also proposed major gas-specific provisions in the draft Petroleum Industry Bill 2012, still pending before the national legislature. The non passage of the bill into law for over a decade has stalled new investments in Nigeria's gas sector. Most of the investments that would have come into Nigeria have gone elsewhere to Nigeria's detriment.

This book considers how Nigeria can achieve energy security in gas, taking into consideration the current challenges in gas production and supply, policies, existing laws and proposed legislation. This book examines the concept of energy security within the context of the Nigerian gas sector, the importance of gas as a resource in Nigeria's economy, the monetization of gas resources in Nigeria, the factors affecting gas utilization in Nigeria, why gas is flared and the impact of gas flaring in Nigeria, the challenge of inadequate gas infrastructure, the competitiveness or otherwise of domestic gas prices, political and international variables affecting gas production and utilization in Nigeria and the adequacy or otherwise of policies and laws to aid security in production and supply of gas in Nigeria.

This book is significant considering that Nigeria's current developmental thrust is hinged on power sector reforms that will succeed only if there is energy security in gas supply. Nigeria currently has an installed power generation capacity of a little over 10,000 Mega Watts, with several additional gas-fired power plants at different stages of completion and many more at the conceptual stage. When these power plants are completed, the demand for gas will increase significantly. Nigeria is yet to achieve 10,000 Mega Watt of power generation due partly to shortage in gas supply.

If there is not enough gas to attain full power generation capacity, then what is the fate of the several on-going and proposed power plant projects? Also, if the supply of gas is not enough to meet the demand within the power sector, what happens to the demand for cooking gas from residential users? Shortage of cooking gas will lead to more reliance on kerosene and wood for fuel, with negative environmental and health effects. The earlier the issue of gas production and supply is sorted out, the better, otherwise Nigeria's vision of becoming one of the 20 developed nations by 2020, will be a mirage.

Elo Adhekpukoli
May 2015

CHAPTER ONE

ENERGY SECURITY IN THE CONTEXT OF NIGERIA's GAS SECTOR

This chapter explains what energy security entails in the context of the Nigerian gas industry. In arriving at a conclusion regarding what energy security entails in Nigeria's gas sector, this chapter first identifies the different perspectives of energy security postulated by scholars and experts and the national and regional geopolitical underpinnings of energy security

1.1   Different Perspectives on Energy Security

Nuttall and Manz[1] identified interruption of the energy supply as the primary threat that faces global energy security.

Borok, Agandu and Morgan[2] view energy security as the availability of energy resources that are diverse, sustainable in quantities, affordable in prices, supports economic growth, assists in poverty alleviation measures, does not harm the environment and that takes note of shocks and disruptions. Energy security has been framed primarily around availability and access to fossil fuels.

For Jum'ah,[3] global energy security is viewed by various stakeholders in different ways, depending on their interests and objectives. The energy security perspective varies depending upon one's position in the value chain. Jum'ah posits that consumers and energy-intensive industries desire reasonably priced energy on demand and worry about disruptions. Major producing countries consider security of revenue and of demand integral parts of any energy security discussion. Upstream operators consider access to new reserves, ability to develop new infrastructure, and stable investment regimes to be critical to ensuring energy security. Developing countries are concerned about the ability to pay for resources to drive their economies and fear balance of payment shocks. Electricity companies are concerned with the integrity of the entire network. Policy makers focus on security of infrastructure, security of supply, security of revenue, access to new reserves, supply diversity, prices, the risks of supply disruption due to terrorism, restiveness, war or natural disaster.

The International Energy Agency (IEA) [4] defines energy security as the uninterrupted availability of energy resources at an affordable

[1] William J. Nuttall and Devon L. Manz,'*A New Energy Security Paradigm for the Twenty-First Century*' Judge Business School, University of Cambridge, 2006 p.3

[2] Maren Borok, Agontu Agandu and Mangai Morgan, '*Energy Security in Nigeria: Challenges and Way Forward*' International Journal of Engineering Science Innovation, Volume 2 Issue 11, November, 2013.

[3] Abdallah S. Jum'ah 'A Perspective on Energy Security' in 'The New Energy Security Paradigm' 2006

[4]   International   Energy   Agency,   'Energy   Security'

price. According to the IEA, energy security has many aspects: long-term energy security and short-term energy security. Long-term energy security mainly deals with timely investments to supply energy in line with economic developments and environmental needs. On the other hand, short-term energy security focuses on the ability of the energy system to react promptly to sudden changes in the supply-demand balance.

According to Davey[5], in a paper presented to the British Parliament in November 2012, there is no perfect definition of energy security. Energy security is a complex issue and any definition must be flexible. Davey explained that when discussing energy security government is primarily concerned about ensuring that consumers have access to the energy services they need (physical security) at prices that avoid excessive volatility (price security).

Fiott, Yamba, Kantu and Iwinjak[6] adopted a broader definition of energy security. According to these scholars, energy security implies that a state, region and/or continent have secure, sustainable, affordable and diversified supplies of renewable and non-renewable energy. A lack of energy security can influence economic productivity, in turn impacting upon the capacity for achieving development goals, the maintenance of livelihoods through economic growth and social and environmental well-being.

Brown, Rewey and Gagliano[7] defined energy security as a resilient energy system. According to these scholars, this resilient system would be capable of withstanding threats through a combination of active, direct security measures – such as surveillance and guards – and passive or more indirect measures such as redundancy,

http://www.iea.org/topics/energysecurity last accessed on February 9, 2015

[5] Edward Davey, Secretary of State for Energy and Climate Change 'Energy Security Strategy' Department of Energy and Climate Change, November 2012, presented to Parliament by the Secretary of State for Energy and Climate Change by Command of Her Majesty

[6] Daniel Fiott, Patrice Yamba T. Kantu and Florian Peter Iwinjak, 'Energy Security' published in 'Climate Change and Security in Africa' Vulnerability Discussion Paper

[7] Matthew H. Brown, Christie Rewey and Troy Gagliano 'Energy Security' April 2003, National Conference of State Legislatures (NCSL)

duplication of critical equipment, diversity in fuel, other sources of energy, and reliance on less vulnerable infrastructure.

Florian Baumann[8] is of the view that energy security is more than sustainability, competitiveness and secure supply. Baumann describes energy security as a multidimensional concept, including external as well as internal action.[9] Economic, political and security measures have to be applied in combination to generate the essential synergies. Any longer interruption of a steady and plenty flow of energy would massively harm a nation's economic output, political stability and the personal wellbeing of its citizens. According to Baumann, societies, especially European societies are entirely addicted to energy services, such as gas stations or electricity. Not only private households, but also the business sector and even public authorities and government agencies are in the dire need of energy to function properly. Hence a satisfactory supply with energy is a precondition for economic growth and legitimacy within a political entity.[10]

1.2 Energy security in the context of national and regional geopolitics

The World Economic Forum[11] defines energy security in the context of political economy. According to the World Economic Forum, energy security is an umbrella term that covers many concerns linking energy, economic growth and political power.

Yergin[12] also posits that the concept of energy security varies from country to country depending on factors and circumstances peculiar to them. According to Yergin, in developed countries, the usual definition of energy security is simply the availability of sufficient supplies at affordable prices. Yergin explained that energy-exporting countries focus on maintaining the 'security of demand' for their

---

[8]Florian Baumann *'Energy Security as multidimensional concept'* Research Group on European Affairs, Centre for Applied Policy (CAP) Research March 2008
[9] ibid
[10] Supra, see note 8 above
[11] World Economic Forum in partnership with Cambridge Energy Research Associates, 'The New Energy Security Paradigm' 2006
[12] Daniel Yergin, *'Ensuring Energy Security'* Council of Foreign Relations 2006

exports, which after all generate the overwhelming share of their government revenue.

Yergin explains that for Russia, the aim is to re-assert state control over strategic resources and gain primacy over the main pipelines and market channels through which it ships its hydrocarbons to international markets.[13]

For China and India, energy security now lies in their ability to rapidly adjust to their new dependence on global markets, which represents a major shift away from their former commitments to self-sufficiency.[14]

For Japan, it means off-setting its stark scarcity of domestic resources through diversification, trade, and investment. In Europe, the concern is on how to manage dependence on imported natural gas – and in most countries, aside from France and Finland, whether to build new nuclear power plants or return to (clean) coal.'[15]

Davey[16] explained that for Britain, securing energy services should not be limited to securing energy supplies, but mean delivering the end products that consumers need: heat, power and transport. According to Davey, energy security especially in the context of Britain's needs should be considered in the context of Britain's other energy objectives of sustainable energy supplies (in particular reducing carbon emissions) and affordable energy supplies.[17]

In the United States, Brown, Rewey and Gagliano[18] explained that energy security focuses on critical infrastructure because the energy system has evolved into one piece of a complex web of infrastructure in the United States. For example, water pumps rely on electricity to operate. Electricity relies on compressed gas as a fuel, which in turn often relies on electricity to run the compressors.

---

[13] ibid
[14] ibid
[15] Ibid
[16] Supra, note 5
[17] Supra, see note 5
[18] Supra, see note 7

Telecommunications systems serve as vital support system from the power grid and they too require electricity. The United State's new high-tech economy demands reliable, petroleum-and electricity based energy system to meet its needs. Disruptions in the manufacturing, distribution and marketing of petroleum-based fuels (including natural gas) could also affect the viability of the transportation system.[19]

The issue of energy security in Europe is quite complex. Europe as a whole is a major importer of natural gas. Europe's natural gas consumption is projected to grow while its own domestic natural gas production continues to decline. If trends continue as projected, Europe's dependence on Russia as a supplier is likely to grow. And, while it could be in Europe's interest to explore alternative sources for its natural gas needs, it is uncertain whether Europe as a whole can, or is willing to, replace significant levels of imports from Russia.[20] Europe as a major energy consumer faces a number of challenges when addressing future energy needs. Among these challenges are rapidly rising global demand and competition for energy resources from emerging economies such as China and India, persistent instability in energy producing regions such as the Middle East, a fragmented internal European energy market, and a growing need to shift fuels in order to address climate change policy.[21]

Over the past decade, some European officials have become increasingly concerned about the potential for cutoffs or curtailments of Russian natural gas supplies to Europe. At least until recently, most Russian natural gas exports to Europe flowed through Ukraine and Belarus. Fragile and sometimes hostile relations between these countries have in the past resulted in interruptions in the flow of natural gas to parts of Europe.[22] Some countries in Eastern Europe,

---

[19] Supra, see note 7
[20] Michael Ratner, Paul Belkin, Jim Nichol, Steven Woehrel, 'Europe's Energy Security: Options and Challenges to Natural Gas Supply Diversification' August 20, 2013, Congressional Research Service (CRS) Report for Congress
[21] ibid
[22] In the mid and late 2000s, many European countries suffered several unexpected energy cut offs due to confrontations between Russia and the key pipeline transit states of Ukraine and Belarus over natural gas supply and transit issues. In 2009, Gazprom halted all natural gas supplies transiting Ukraine for nearly three weeks

which are in some cases almost exclusively reliant on Russian gas imports, have been particularly susceptible to these fluctuations.

In response to past supply cutoffs and the potential for future energy supply interruptions, European leaders, sometimes with the support of the United States, have sought to increase their energy security by exploring supply diversification options.[23] Russia and some Western European countries also responded to these incidents by planning new pipeline projects to bypass what they viewed as problematic transit states. One new natural gas pipeline is the Nord Stream pipeline under the Baltic Sea, which transports natural gas from Russia to Germany. While building pipelines that circumvent Ukraine, Russia continues its long-standing efforts to gain control of Ukraine's pipeline system. Some Russian actions may be aimed at frustrating European efforts at diversification. These include trying to sign long-term contracts with Azerbaijan and Central Asian states to lock up supplies sought by the Europeans; lodging legal objections to the proposed Trans-Caspian Pipeline between Azerbaijan and

---

after the two sides failed to reach agreement on several issues, including a debt allegedly owed by Ukraine to Gazprom and the price that Ukraine would pay for natural gas supplies. In 2010 and 2011, disputes between Russia and Belarus over a variety of issues, including energy prices, debts owed by Belarus, and transit fees paid by Russia for the use of Belarusian pipelines, led to temporary reductions of oil and natural gas supplies to Belarus and neighbouring countries.

[23] One such response, though contrary to the US perspective of energy security through diversification, has been the decision by some EU members to support construction of the Nord Stream pipeline, which directly connects Russia and Germany, Russia's largest importer. Russia has also committed to building the South Stream pipeline across the Black Sea, connecting Russia, Bulgaria, and Hungary. While these pipeline projects bypass transit states such as Ukraine and Belarus, they also bypass EU member states like Poland and Lithuania that are more critical of Russian policies. The Russian-backed projects are also widely seen as rivals to other pipelines supported by the EU. A second EU response to concerns over Europe's reliance on Russian natural gas supplies is what has become known as the Southern strategy of the Southern Corridor to transport natural gas from the Caspian region and Central Asia. Although the long-time centerpiece of this strategy, the proposed Nabucco natural gas pipeline, is no longer considered a commercially viable project, it has been replaced by the planned smaller-scale Trans-Anatolian natural gas pipeline (TANAP), which would connect to the Trans Adriatic Pipeline (TAP), which goes from the Turkish border through Greece and Albania, and ends in Italy. Nabucco West, the rival of TAP, would have transported natural gas from Turkey's western border to Austria.

Turkmenistan, which would be a key link in providing Caspian gas to Europe; and attempting to coordinate natural gas export policies with other leading producers such as Qatar and Iran.

1.3   Energy security in the context of Nigeria's gas sector

The concept of energy security is not new to the Nigerian government. Former Nigerian President, Olusegun Obasanjo[24] in his foreword to the proceedings of the Energy Policy Conference held in 1978 declared that "Energy, in all its ramifications, has finally emerged in our consciousness as a crucial element in this unavoidable industrialization and socio-economic development process."

Energy security in the context of the Nigerian gas sector is a two-pronged approach – security of demand for Nigerian gas in the international gas market, and security of supply of gas for the domestic market to drive economic development and sector reforms, especially in electricity generation, deforestation through increased use of Liquefied Petroleum Gas (LPG), agriculture through development of fertilizer plants and other gas-based industries.

According to Yergin[25] the key to energy security for energy importers is diversification of energy suppliers. Applying this concept to energy exporters like Nigeria, the key to Nigeria's energy security is the diversification of foreign buyers for her energy resources and therefore achieving security of demand.

Energy security in Nigeria from the civilian regime of Olusegun Obasanjo since 1999, to the Goodluck Jonathan administration has taken a more robust dimension. Whereas, earlier governments had treated the energy sector exclusively as a foreign exchange earner, Olusegun Obasanjo regarded the sector as a potential driver of development through capacity building in human and infrastructural

---

[24] Chidi Orazulike, 'Energy Crisis: The Bane of Nigeria's Development,' Oilgas Magazine, December 12, 2013, cited in Maren Borok et al *'Energy Security in Nigeria: Challenges and Way Forward'* International Journal of Engineering Science Innovation, Volume 2 Issue 11, November, 2013.

[25] Supra, see note 12

development. Olusegun Obasanjo initiated the idea of awarding oil and gas blocks to foreign companies in exchange for commitments to develop infrastructure. Olusegun Obasanjo also initiated the National Energy Policy of 2003.

The National Energy Policy[26] has as one of its objectives, the development of Nigeria's energy resources, with diversified energy resources option, for the achievement of national energy security. Nigeria also aims to promote the development and adoption of energy efficient methods in energy utilization to enhance security and self reliance. Nigeria is also involved in bilateral, regional and international arrangements to complement domestic efforts towards energy security for the nation. Nigeria, as a policy, is engaged in promoting favourable trading relationships with member countries of Economic Community of West African States (ECOWAS) and the African Union (AU) for easy distribution of petroleum and gas in the region.

---

[26] The Presidency, Federal Republic of Nigeria, Energy Commission 'National Energy Policy' 2003

CHAPTER TWO

THE IMPORTANCE OF GAS AS AN ENERGY RESOURCE IN NIGERIA

This chapter explains the role gas plays in the Nigerian economy. The utilization of gas both for domestic use and as export commodity, and the factors affecting gas utilization in Nigeria are discussed in this chapter.

Gas was hitherto regarded as the fuel of the future but the reality is that gas is fast becoming the preferred fuel for today because of its advanced thermal efficiency, clean combustion characteristics and the significant amounts of undeveloped gas worldwide. Nigeria has the largest gas reserves in Africa with proven reserves of about 184 Trillion cubit feet (Tcf) of gas.[27] Nigeria is however ranked third amongst African countries in terms of gas production, with production level currently at about 8 Billion cubic feet (Bcf) per day.[28] It is safe to conclude that at current production levels, Nigeria is not likely to exhaust its proven reserves of about 184 Tcf for many years to come, even if no new reserves are discovered.

2.1   Domestic gas utilization

Nigeria utilizes gas for electricity generation, cooking in residential houses and for industrial purposes such as production of methanol and fertilizer.

a. Electricity generation

Nigeria relies largely on gas for electricity generation and this will continue to be so until other sources of energy are developed. Without gas Nigeria would be in almost total darkness. Nigeria currently generates electricity through hydro power and gas. Hydro power accounts for less than 20% of the installed power generation capacity in Nigeria, while gas accounts for the rest. The combined hydro-power generation capacity of the Kainji, Shiroro and Jebba hydro power stations in Nigeria is only about 1,938 Mega Watts (MW). Before the privatisation of government-owned gas-fired power generating plants under President Goodluck Jonathan, the Federal Government-owned gas-fired power plants had a combined generating capacity of about 4,261 Mega Watts (MW). The 10 new gas fired plants constructed between 2003 and 2015 under the National Integrated Power Project (NIPP) jointly by the Federal,

---

[27] Funsho Kupolokun, 'Nigeria and the future gas market', a lecture delivered by the then Group Managing Director of the Nigerian National Petroleum Corporation at the Baker Institute Energy Forum, Rice University, 2006.
[28] NNPC Articles, 'Nigeria to Support EU Long Term Gas Supply Security', www.nnpcgroup.com/PublicRelations/NNPCinthenews/tabid/92/articleType/ArticleView/articleId/537/Nigeria-to-Support-EU-Long-Term-Gas-Supply-Security.aspx. last accessed on 8th April, 2015.

State and Local Governments, had a combined generating capacity of 5,033 Mega Watts.

Security of gas supply for power generation is determined by adequate gas pipeline infrastructure to connect all the gas-fired power stations to gas producing fields. Security of gas supply for power generation is also determined by competitive gas pricing and compliance with payments schedules. Gas producers in Nigeria preferred to export gas rather than sell to power generating stations at a loss as a result of low domestic prices. Gas producers also preferred to export gas due to consistent default in payments by the now defunct government owned power utility company. The Power Holding Company of Nigeria (PHCN) before it was recently unbundled and privatized in 2013, had an outstanding debt in excess of N23 billion (Twenty Three Billion Naira) as at 2012, for gas purchased from gas producers. The availability of gas for power generation will also be determined by new investments in upstream gas production. According to Austin Avuru's[29] prediction in 2013 of Nigeria's inability to meet its proposed target of a supply of about 3 Bcf of gas per day to the power sector has become a reality. According to Avuru, Nigeria produced about 3.8 Bcf per day of gas in 2011 out of which 70% was exported, leaving only 1.14 Bcf per day for domestic use, including power. Based on the target of about a supply of 3 Bcf per day of gas for the existing power generating plants by 2015, the power sector would suffer a shortfall of about 1.86 Bcf per day of gas supply by 2015. The incentives required to boost investments in gas exploration and production never came. Instead investors have had to deal with so much uncertainty surrounding the proposed Petroleum Industry Bill.

b. Cooking gas for residential use

Nigeria is the 6th largest global producer of LPG and 2nd largest producer of LPG in Africa. Nigeria, unfortunately and surprisingly so, has the lowest LPG consumption average in West Africa. The

---

[29] Austin Avuru, 'Strategies for Sustaining Gas to Power Agenda for Economic and Industrial Growth: The Upstream Point of View: What incentive to invest when demand is unsure?' published in Nigerian Gas Journal of the Nigerian Gas Association, *Insights into Nigeria's Gas Revolution* Half Year Edition 2013

demand for LPG in Nigeria is restricted by affordability of cylinders, effective distribution channels, awareness, wrong perception of gas as a dangerous cooking fuel, culture and economic reasons.[30] Global LPG consumption as at 2013 was 265 Million Tonnes[31]. Nigeria consumed about 0.12 Metric tonnes in 2012. The average LPG consumption per person annually in North Africa is 53 kilograms, and 2.5 kilograms(kg) in sub-Sahara Africa. Nigeria currently has an average LPG consumption of 0.8kilograms (kg) per person annually.

LPG is commonly known in Nigeria as cooking gas even though it is also used as automotive fuel for vehicles in some developed countries. According to the World LP Gas Association,[32] over 15 million vehicles run on LPG in Europe and Eurasia and there are over 23 million of such vehicles in the world as at 2013. Nigeria has no current plans to utilize LPG as automotive fuel like other developed countries have done.

Some of the advantages of LPG over other fuels include the following:

- Weight and portability- Though heavier than air, LPG is approximately just half the weight of water, thus making it easier to be stored in pressure cylinders and tanks and hence, could easily be transported over long distances.
- Cleaner- LPG burns cleanly and virtually without any soot as it mixes completely with air, which creates a perfect combustion with low carbon and sulphur emissions.
- Odourless- Compared to other fuels, LPG is an odourless fuel. However, some suppliers usually add odorants in order for leakages to be easily perceived and detected.
- Non toxic- LPG is non toxic. Prolonged and sudden exposure to it in reasonable quantity could however, cause cold burns and suffocation.

---

[30] Abayomi Awobokun, *Developing the Domestic LPG Market: Challenges and Prospects, July 20*, 2012. A presentation made at the *Centre for Petroleum Information(CPI) 12th Petroleum Policy Round Table tagged: 'Making the Gas Revolution Happen'*
[31] Argus Media Limited, *Statistical Review of Global LP Gas, 2013.*
[32] World LP Gas Association *Annual Report 2013.*

- Cheaper- Compared to other fuels and even electricity, LPG is more cost effective.
- Complexity and maintenance- LPG installations are less complicated, easy to maintain and even requires less maintenance.

Nigeria's storage infrastructure for LPG is still underutilized largely because of indifference by consumers, inadequate supply from refineries and lack of connecting pipelines to inland storage depots. The Nigeria National Petroleum Corporation (NNPC) has 9 inland LPG storage depots with a combined capacity of 12,000 metric tonnes located at Ibadan, Ilorin, Enugu, Gusau, Gombe, Makurdi, Calabar and Kano. The NNPC also has 2 coastal LPG depots, the Apapa depot (4,000 metric tonnes) and Calabar depot (1,000 metric tonnes). The Calabar depot has, however, been concessioned to a private indigenous gas company. The Nigeria Liquefied Natural Gas Limited (NLNG) has 4 LPG tanks (65,000 cubic meters each). Total Nigeria has a storage facility at Apapa, while Ascon, NIPCO and NNPC are constructing 3 new LPG storage facilities all at Apapa.

Security of LPG supply in the domestic market will not likely be achieved without linking the LPG inland depots through pipelines to the gas fields and processing facilities and many homes will continue to rely on fuel wood and kerosene for cooking. There is currently no known serious effort by the Nigerian government to construct connecting pipelines to all the inland LPG depots. LPG consumers in non-coastal states therefore have to depend on inter-state LPG trucks for supply of LPG. The plans of the Nigerian government to increase the consumption of LPG across the country will likely remain a mirage as long as the inland LPG storage depots remain idle and isolated.

c. Gas based industries

Some industries rely on gas as feedstock such as fertilizer and methanol production, while some others require gas to provide the energy required to operate plants and machinery. Industries and factories in Nigeria are beginning to switch from diesel oil to gas for their operations because gas is more environmentally friendly and cheaper in the long-term. The result is increase in demand for gas.

Nigeria has experienced investments in the cement manufacturing sector in recent times, which has led to Nigeria becoming a net exporter of cement.[33] Specifically, Nigeria's cement output capacity increased from 2 million metric tonnes in 2002 to 28.5 million metric tonnes in 2013.[34] The cement factories rely mostly on gas for their production. The major gas consumers for cement production are Larfarge/WAPCO, Ashaka Cement, Dangote Cement and Obajana Cement.

The fertilizer industry in Nigeria is also expected to experience increase in demand for fertilizer by 6 to 7 % every year over the next 20 years.[35] The current major producer of fertilizer in Nigeria is Notore Chemical Industries. The Dangote Group has also concluded plans with Siapem SPA to build a fertilizer plant. Nagarjuna Fertilizers & Chemicals Limited and Indorama also have plans to build fertilizer plants in Nigeria. The increase in the number of fertilizer plants in Nigeria will result in increase in demand for gas supply.

The petrochemical industry is also a major domestic consumer of gas in Nigeria. Gas is a major feedstock of the petrochemical industry. Xenel plans to build a new petrochemical plant in Nigeria in addition to the existing petrochemical companies.

The iron and steel industry in Nigeria is moribund. The inactivity of these steel mills has reduced the gas consumption for iron and steel

---

[33] Okonjo Iweala, 'Transforming the Nigerian Economy: Opportunities and Challenges' 2014 Convocation Address delivered by the Co-ordinating Minister for the Economy and Hon. Minister of Finance at Babcock University, June, 2014. http://www.fmf.gov.ng/departments/economic-research-and-policy-management/190-transforming-the-nigerian-economy-opportunities-and-challenges.html last accessed on 8th April, 2015

[34] ibid

[35] Ukpohor Excel 'Nigerian Gas Master Plan: Strengthening The Nigeria Gas Infrastructure Blueprint As A Base For Expanding Regional Gas Market,' a technical paper delivered at the World Gas Conference 2009

production to near zero. If Nigeria is able to get her major steel mills rolling again, the demand for gas supply will certainly increase.

2.2 Export gas utilization

Higher gas prices in the international market continue to create a preferential pull for gas exports. Gas producers in Nigeria have therefore developed a disproportionate focus for gas exports to the detriment of domestic gas supply. This has resulted in a significant shortfall in the availability of gas for domestic utilization.

a. Liquefied natural gas

Nigeria commenced export of liquefied natural gas in 1999 with the export of the first LNG cargo on October 9, 1999 to Enel of Italy at Montoir LNG terminal in France. The NLNG mops up gas that would otherwise be flared. The NLNG between 1999 and 2013, converted about 4.2 Tcf of associated gas to export Liquefied Natural Gas and Natural Gas Liquid products, which otherwise would have been flared.[36] The NLNG currently delivers about 8% of the world's LNG supply. The NLNG has 16 (sixteen) long term LNG Sales Purchase Agreements (SPAs) executed with 11 buyers spread across the Atlantic and Pacific basins.[37] The NLNG has made significant contributions to Nigeria's income, delivering over $13 billion US dollars as dividends to Nigeria in the last thirteen years.[38]

b. Liquefied petroleum gas and condensates

Nigeria also exports LPG and condensates. The NLNG made its first shipment of condensate cargo on April 4, 2000. The NNPC/Exxon Mobil OSO Condensate Project produces refrigerated propane and butane for export at Bonny Island. Nigeria actually exports more LPG than it consumes locally. The NLNG made its first shipment of LPG on June 25, 2003.

---

[36] Nigeria Liquefied Natural Gas Limited, 'Facts & Figures on NLNG 2014'
[37] ibid
[38] ibid

c. Automotive natural gas diesel

Nigeria commenced production of automotive natural gas diesel in September 2014 through the Chevron Escravos Gas to Liquid (EGTL) project. Nigeria plans to export natural gas diesel fuel used by vehicles in some developed countries. The product will not be utilized locally because the vehicles in Nigeria use premium motor spirit and diesel fuel from crude oil and do not use natural gas as fuel.

2.3 Factors affecting gas utilization in Nigeria

There are various factors affecting the effective utilization of gas in Nigeria. The factors include but are not limited to, the expensive nature of gas production, limited local demand, inadequate gas pipeline infrastructure, low gas pricing, and the sophistication in the gas export market. These factors currently threaten Nigeria's energy security in gas.

a. Expensive nature of gas production

Gas is usually not sold in its raw form, unlike crude oil, which can be sold in its raw form right from the well head. Gas requires some processing into different variants, just like the process of refining crude oil into different products. The gathering and processing of the gas involves separating, isolating and removing the heavier hydrocarbon compounds before delivery to the end user. This process is very expensive and discouraging to most oil producers who are more interested oil. The gas producer will also incur more costs in the case of associated gas. Associated gas would have to be separated from the crude oil first, before it is processed. The production of gas therefore implies additional investment in gas processing facilities by the producer.

b. Limited domestic demand

The domestic gas market for a long time could only absorb a relatively small percentage of gas produced daily. Local demand has however been on the increase in recent times with the development of more gas based industries and gas-fired power plants. A lot still needs to be done especially in the domestic use of LPG for cooking. Nigerians rely more on kerosene for cooking rather than LPG, which is a better, safer, cheaper and more environmentally friendly option.

c. Inadequate gas pipeline infrastructure

Domestic gas transportation through pipelines is more economically efficient and safer than the use of trucks. Before the Nigeria Gas Company (NGC) was established in 1988, inadequate pipeline network for gas transportation was a major factor that adversely affected gas utilization in Nigeria. Most companies requiring gas were unfortunately isolated from gas supply due to the inadequate pipeline infrastructure in the country. As stated earlier, the various LPG depots scattered all over the country are adversely affected by inadequate pipeline infrastructure. Most of the inland LPG depots are isolated from gas supply, which accounts partly for the low utilization of LPG in Nigeria. The utilization of gas for power generation has also suffered much due to inadequate pipeline infrastructure connecting the power plants to the gas fields. For example, most of the NIPP stations built under President Olusegun Obasanjo, between 2003 and 2007, could not commence power generation upon completion because there were no pipelines to supply the gas required to generate electricity. President Goodluck Jonathan however did a lot to construct gas pipelines to connect most of the NIPP stations. This puts Nigeria in a good position to attain energy security in gas supply to the domestic market.

d. Low gas pricing

The global market price of gas is very low when compared to the global market price of crude oil. For example, natural gas price has averaged $3.93 US dollars from 1990 until April 2015, reaching an all time high of $15.39US dollars in December 2005 and a record low of $1.02US dollars per million British thermal unit (MMBtu) in January, 1992. [39] The current average price for natural gas as at April, 2015, is $2.67US dollars per MMBtu.[40]

Crude oil price on the other hand has averaged $39.89 US dollars per Barrel from 1946 till 2015, reaching an all time high of $145.31 US dollars per Barrel.[41] The current average price for crude oil as at

---

[39] Trading Economics, http://www.tradingeconomics.com/commodity/natural-gas last accessed on 8th April, 2015
[40] ibid

April, 2015, is $53.95US dollars per Barrel.[42] Considering that a barrel of crude oil is equivalent to 5.8 MMBtu of natural gas,[43] it follows that trading in oil is more profitable than trade in natural gas.

The global pricing of oil and gas is largely affected by the economics of scale. Crude oil is still the major source of energy globally and has the largest market share when compared to other sources of energy. The world practically runs on crude oil, that is, the various refined products of crude oil such as premium motor spirit, aviation fuel, diesel oil and kerosene. Nigeria has very low refining capacity for crude oil, from which she derives much of her export revenue.

All it takes to export crude oil is to pump the crude oil from the ground, transport it to the ocean going tankers for delivery to buyers. Trade in crude oil is therefore simpler than trade in natural gas, which requires the establishment of sophisticated and expensive infrastructure for gathering, processing and transportation of gas. Oil producers are therefore likely to derive more and quicker profit from the sale of crude oil than natural gas. Industry players in Nigeria have therefore focused more on trading crude oil for quick profit rather than investing in gas development, which requires mostly long-term investments.

e. Sophisticated gas export market

Nigeria is far from the major developed gas markets in the world. Gas is more difficult to export than crude oil. The global gas export market is very sophisticated, when compared to the global crude oil export market. Gas exported by sea must first be liquefied and thereafter transported through specially built LNG tankers. At the delivery terminal, a regasification facility is required to convert the liquefied gas to gaseous state again. Gas export by sea therefore

---

[41] Trading Economics http://www.tradingeconomics.com/commodity/crude-oil last accessed on 8th April, 2015
[42] ibid
[43] Iowa State University, *Liquid Fuel Measurements and Conversions'* October 2008. https://www.extension.iastate.edu/agdm/wholefarm/pdf/c6-87.pdf last accessed 8th April, 2015.

entails the construction of liquefaction plants, refrigerated LNG Ocean going tankers and regasification plant. This is no little investment in terms of money. The cost of building an LNG tanker is also very high, when compared to oil tankers. This is because LNG tankers must be specially equipped to keep the gas refrigerated at 160^0c at all times.

Gas can also be exported in its gaseous state through underground pipelines. This requires the construction of trans-border pipelines with the numerous local and international legal, socio-economic and political challenges associated with such projects. The construction of the proposed Trans-Saharan Gas pipeline, targeted at supplying Nigerian gas to Europe is yet to commence. Nigeria therefore had to invest heavily in LNG Tankers to become a player in the world gas market. In Africa for example, Algeria is better positioned to supply gas to Europe. Algeria will incur lesser cost exporting gas to Europe than Nigeria.

Nigeria could not establish herself in the world gas market until 2001, when she made her first LNG shipment. The West-African sub-regional market where Nigeria can establish its unrivalled dominance is still undeveloped. The West African Gas Pipeline project was completed in 2009. The pipeline was constructed mainly to export Nigerian gas to Ghana. Togo and the Republic of Benin, the two other countries involved in the project, are not major gas markets for Nigeria.

While crude oil has well developed spot markets, it is very difficult to sell natural gas in a spot market. Crude oil can be produced with no buyer in mind. The oil producer produces the oil, and easily finds a vessel to transport the oil. This is because there are numerous oil tankers in the world because of the huge investments in ocean going crude oil tankers for the haulage of crude oil. The crude oil is transported to a location where a buyer could be found on the spot. Negotiations are concluded and the oil is off-loaded to the buyer or transported to any destination of the buyer's choice.

It is not so with natural gas. LNG tankers are very few in the world when compared to the numerous crude oil tankers. Most LNG tankers are in fact owned by gas producing companies who use such tankers to transport their own gas to customers. A gas producer without its own LNG tanker will therefore face the uphill task of first finding a vessel to transport the gas produced. The gas producer would then face another uphill task of finding a buyer to take the gas. In addition, gas sales and purchase agreements are usually long term, usually between 10 – 20years between a gas producer and the buyer. This is unlike the sale of crude oil which can be negotiated on the spot.

CHAPTER THREE

POLICY MEASURES FOR ENERGY SECURITY IN NIGERIA's GAS SECTOR

Over the years, successive Nigerian government regimes have introduced different policies geared towards maximizing Nigeria's gas resource. The various policy measures are discussed in this chapter.

3.1   Associated Gas Re-Injection

Nigeria introduced a gas re-injection policy for associated gas in 1979. The gas re-injection policy was the first major policy measure aimed at reducing flaring of associated gas produced in the process of drilling for crude oil. The policy culminated in the enactment of the Associated Gas Re-injection Act, 1979. Oil producing companies were required to re-inject the associated gas into the reservoir rather than resorting to flaring. There is, however, no gas re-injection policy for non-associated gas. There was no need for a gas re-injection policy for non-associated gas because the production of non-associated gas implied that the producing company already had plans for utilization of the non-associated gas produced and there was therefore no incidence of flaring non-associated gas.

By re-injecting unutilized gas, Nigeria's gas resources were preserved for future exploitation rather than being wasted through gas flaring. This was one of the first steps towards energy security in Nigeria's gas sector considering the fact that gas is not a renewable energy resource.

3.2   Butanization policy

Nigeria introduced the butanization policy in the 1980s to encourage the use of LPG as cooking fuel as a measure towards increasing gas utilization and also to address the problem of deforestation and desertification. The butanization programme included the introduction of large quantitites of new cylinders, retail price control of LPG, distribution of gas stoves, enhanced production of LPG especially at the Kaduna refinery, and construction of strategically located LPG storage depots around the country.[44] As mentioned earlier, the Nigerian government constructed nine LPG depots in different parts of the country. The depots were commissioned in the mid-1990s, and LPG supply was expected from the four oil refineries in the country. The government controlled LPG prices until the LPG

---

[44] The World Bank, *The Nigerian LP Gas Sector Improvement Study, March 2004.* Energy Sector Management Assistance Programme (ESMAP) Report

market was deregulated in 1998 and price control was officially brought to an end.[45]

The butanization policy began to fail in its early days and seems never to have recovered since then. Apart from the butanization policy, all other policy measures towards gas utilization have been largely successful and enjoyed continuity by successive administrations in Nigeria. Certain factors led to the ultimate failure of the butanization policy. Firstly, LPG marketers began to cut back on investment in cylinders due to inflation. Nigeria is still in the throes of shortage of gas cylinders, which means that very few households utilize LPG for cooking. Secondly, soon after the commissioning of the nine inland LPG depots, the four refineries suffered successive shut downs. This led to large scale importation of LPG. Nigeria depended mainly on importation of LPG for most of its domestic demand, until 2007 when the NLNG commenced supply of LPG to the domestic market. Thirdly, there was no sustainable plan in place to transport LPG to the inland depots. Much reliance was placed on road trucks rather than the more efficient pipeline transportation system. The initial idea of the government was to build the inland depots close to the rail lines. The Nigerian railway system has been very inefficient and never really played a significant role in the transportation of LPG to the inland depots. The result is that only the two coastal depots in Lagos and Calabar are functional. Supply to these two coastal depots is however affected by congestions at the ports and the priority given to competing fuels on the loading and discharging berths.

The failure of the butanization policy impacts negatively on Nigeria's quest for energy security in gas supply to the domestic market. The intention of the government was that the inland depots will aid the widespread utilization of LPG for cooking by making the product easily accessible to more Nigerians in the hinterland. The isolation of the inland depots has therefore impacted negatively on the utilization of LPG. The LPG sector will experience speedy revival if these inland depots that have been lying idle for about 20 years running, are brought on stream. Unfortunately, there seems to be no serious

---

[45] ibid

policy focus on leveraging on the investments of previous government regimes in constructing the inland depots. The Nigerian Gas Master Plan 2008 aimed at consolidating on the gains of the pre-2008 government policy measures on gas utilization, is silent on the butanization policy. The surprising omission of the LPG sector from the 2008 gas master plan will negatively impact security of LPG supply to the domestic market. This oversight is worth looking into by the Nigerian government.

3.3   The Export Policy

Nigeria has realized the economic potential of gas as a revenue earner. This realisation led to various export projects that have seen gas become the second major export commodity in Nigeria, after crude oil. These projects are discussed below.

a. The Liquefied Natural Gas projects
Nigeria has decided to harness its vast gas resources and become a major player in the global gas market through the export of LNG. LNG is more capital intensive than crude oil trade and requires financing from private financial institutions. Moreover, government could not fund the LNG business alone. Most private financial institutions will not commit the colossal amounts required to fund LNG projects owned by government due to political instability. The failure of an LNG project due to government mismanagement or change in policy has the potential of sinking even the largest of financial institutions. It became necessary therefore for the Nigerian government to cede majority shares in the NLNG to private sector ownership.

The Nigeria LNG Limited was incorporated as a limited liability company on May 17, 1989, with the NNPC (49%), Shell (25.6%), Total LNG Nigeria Limited (15%) and Eni (10.4%). The Nigerian government adopted this ownership structure as a pragmatic approach to developing the LNG business in Nigeria. The Bonny Gas Transport Limited was also established alongside the NLNG to provide shipping capacity for the NLNG project.[46] The NLNG Ship

Manning Limited was also incorporated to develop and train shipboard personnel for the Bonny Gas Transport vessels.[47]

Following the incorporation of the NLNG Limited, the Final Investment Decision for Trains 1 and 2 was executed in November 1995. Construction of the plant commenced in February 1996. By February 1999, the Final Investment Decision for Train 3 was executed. Production commenced on September 15, 1999 and on October 9, 1999, the NLNG exported its 1st LNG cargo. On August 5, 2000, the NLNG exported its 50th LNG cargo. On March 20, 2002, the Final Investment Decision was executed for Trains 4 and 5, and by July 2004, the Final Investment Decision for Train 6 was executed. In December 2006, the NLNG exported its 1,000th LNG cargo. In October 2010, the NLNG exported its 2,000th LNG cargo. On January 17, 2014, the NLNG exported its 3000th cargo. The NLNG currently has a production capacity of 22 million metric tonnes per annum (mmtpa). The NLNG plans to build Train 7 with a capacity of 8.4mmtpa. [48]

The success of the NLNG motivated the Nigerian government and other investors to initiate the Brass LNG and Olokola LNG projects. The initial ownership structure for Brass LNG reflects the following: NNPC (49%), Eni (17%), Conoco Phillips (17%) and Total (17%). Conocco Phillips exited in late 2014 and divested its shareholding to Oando Plc, a Nigerian company. The $3.5 billion US dollars Brass LNG plant project is currently waiting for the Final Investment Decision to be signed for full scale construction to begin. The Olokola LNG plant is under evaluation and will cost $7 billion US dollars. The ownership structure for Olokola LNG reflects the following: NNPC (49.5%), Shell (18.5%), Chevron (18.5%) and British Gas (13.5%). The Brass LNG and Olokola LNG projects have not been as successful as the NLNG due to the exit of key technical partners like Conoco Phillips and British Gas.

The delay in the Olokola and Brass LNG projects does not advance

---

[46] Nigeria Liquefied Natural Gas Limited, 'Facts & Figures on NLNG 2014'
[47] ibid
[48] ibid

Nigeria's quest for energy security in the world gas market. If these projects come on stream, Nigeria will be in a stronger position to increase her market share in the world LNG market.

b. The West African Gas Pipeline Project

The West African Gas Pipeline is the only existing regional gas pipeline through which Nigeria currently exports gas. The pipeline was commissioned on the 13th of May, 2008, and ready for transportation of gas since 14th of December, 2008. The first export of gas through the pipeline was made in December 2008 to Ghana. Nigeria intends to use regional pipelines to supplement its ocean-dependent LNG business. The West African Gas Pipeline has been under utilized so far and Ghana, the major consumer is already considering alternatives to Nigerian gas.[49]

Nigeria's energy security in gas export will be negatively impacted if the West African Gas Pipeline outlives its relevance and becomes redundant.

c. The Trans-Saharan Gas Pipeline project

The Trans-Saharan Gas Pipeline project will run from Nigeria, through Niger to Hassi R'Mel in Algeria, where it will be connected with the existing Algeria export system to supply gas to Europe. The NNPC and Sonatrach signed the Memorandum of Understanding for this project on 4th January, 2002, on behalf of Nigeria and Algeria, respectively. In June 2005, NNPC and Sonatrach signed a contract with Pepsen Limited for a feasibility study of the project which is estimated to cost about $6 billion US dollars. The construction of the pipeline and gathering centres will cost about $15 billion US dollars.[50] Construction work is yet to commence and it is not likely that this project will come on stream in the short term due to political and security issues related to terrorism in Nigeria, Niger and Algeria.

The delay in the Trans-Saharan gas pipeline limits Nigeria's options

---

[49] Infra, see note 143
[50] Ukpohor Excel, *Nigerian Gas Master Plan: Strengthening The Nigeria Gas Infrastructure Blueprint As A Base For Expanding Regional Gas Market*, a technical paper delivered at the World Gas Conference

for gas export to Europe. Nigeria currently exports gas to Coastal European countries through NLNG. The Trans-Saharan gas pipeline would have provided an alternative route for Nigerian gas to Europe without having to undergo the liquefaction and re-gasification processes involved in LNG trade. This negatively affects Nigeria's quest for energy security in the gas export market.

3.4   The Nigerian Gas Master Plan 2008[51]

The Nigerian Gas Master Plan (NGMP) 2008 is the most robust policy put in place so far by the Nigerian government to ensure security of gas supply to Nigeria's domestic market and also ensure Nigeria's capacity to meet export demands from other countries. The gas master plan has the potential to help Nigeria attain energy security in both the domestic and international gas markets.

President, Umaru Yar'Adua approved the Nigerian Gas Master Plan on February 13, 2008, and President Goodluck Jonathan continued with the implementation of the NGMP. The NGMP is a policy framework intended to further strengthen Nigeria's position as a major player in the international gas market and improve domestic utilization of gas for accelerated economic development. The NGMP is a government-led, industry-supported initiative, which was developed, taking into consideration the balance between incentivizing exploration of gas and ensuring security of gas supply. NGMP is anchored on the following 3 (three) point strategic economic development agenda:

Gas to power – Natural gas will be deployed as Nigeria's dominant fuel for power generation, with the objective of attaining increase in power generation capacity to 15,000 MW by 2018 and 20,000 MW by 2020. The gas to power development agenda under the NGMP seeks to consolidate the power sector reforms which started under President Olusegun Obasanjo in year 2000. Nigeria will first need to attain the already existing installed generating capacity of about 10,000MW, up from the current actual generating capacity of about

---

[51] The Presidency, Federal Republic of Nigeria, 'The Nigerian Gas Master Plan 2008'

4,000 MW. This can only be possible through adequate gas supply to the existing and new power generating stations. A further increase in the generating capacity from 10,000MW to 20,000MW will require more power generating stations, and indeed, more gas supply. Without a consistent gas to power policy, the power sector reforms will fail.

Gas Based Industrialization – Nigeria will be positioned as the African regional hub for gas based industries; that is, industries that use natural gas as feedstock, such as fertilizer, petrochemicals and methanol. These primary industries, if properly delivered, will stimulate a wide range of small and medium scale secondary industries that will drive growth in Nigeria's Gross Domestic Product (GDP).

Fertilizer production will boost agricultural yield, causing growth of agro-processing and related industries. Nigeria intends to achieve self sufficiency in fertilizer production to support the agricultural sector. The petrochemical industry will produce polyethylene and polypropylene which are basic ingredients for a wide range of secondary industries such as packaging, plastics and carpets. Nigeria plans to build a new gas industrial park at Ogidigben, Delta State. The industrial park is anchored around the proposed Xenel petrochemical plant, Nagarjuna fertilizer plant and NNPC/Chevron central processing facility.[52]

High Value Export – Nigeria will selectively invest in high value export through LNG and regional gas pipelines. Specifically, as regards LNG, Nigeria will aim to protect about 10% of global market share of LNG trade. It will also leverage its natural gas for regional economic influence by selective investment in cross-country pipelines within the sub-region, stimulating the economic growth of those nations and creating investment and sales outlet opportunities for Nigerian entrepreneurs and for Nigerian gas.

a. The Domestic Gas Supply Obligation[53]

---

[52] David Ige, 'Gas Revolution Agenda: Status Update', published in Nigerian Gas Journal of the Nigerian Gas Association, *Insights into Nigeria's Gas Revolution* Half Year Edition 2013

The primary objective of the Domestic Supply Obligation (DSO) policy is to jumpstart gas supply availability to a level that will enable immediate response to the rapid growth in demand from power plants, create a base load of gas supply that would enable diversification of the market and jumpstart industrialization; and provide sufficient supply to underpin the commercial development of the extensive pipeline infrastructure required to support the market. The DSO requires all associated and non-associated gas reserves holders to dedicate a specific volume of gas supply to the domestic market based upon their gas reserves, their total production and their levels of flaring.

The DSO policy is a transitional policy intervention aimed at driving supply availability, in the short term, to a level that would sustainably support a fully competitive gas market. During the transition and subject to the Federal Ministry of Petroleum Resources (FMPR) subsequent assessment of the state of the nation's requirement;

- All oil and gas suppliers in the country will be mandated to set aside a certain amount of pre-allocated volume of gas for the domestic gas market;

- The mandatory obligation will be for a fixed volume of gas contributing to an overall base load determined by the FMPR for the purpose of transitioning the market only;

- Beyond this initial allocation, supply growth will be on a 'willing buyer, willing seller' basis, but the FMPR will retain the right to impose additional obligations, if considered necessary to do so in the interest of the nation;

- The DSO will be deployed for specific strategic purposes towards transitioning the market rapidly. This includes but not limited to, achieving a diversified off-take across sectors (power, industries, e.t.c.), and stimulating the growth of backbone gas infrastructure across the country;

- The DSO will be administered centrally in order to ensure that Nigeria's strategic objectives for the transition are realized. The gas aggregation company was therefore established to manage the DSO;

---

[53] Supra, see note 51

- Supporting commercial policies will be developed to assure commercial viability of the supply;
- Suppliers who meet their obligation will be able to supply excess gas above the DSO on a 'willing buyer, willing seller' basis;
- The obligation will be set based on a target 5-year realization frame

b. Gas Pricing Policy[54]

The gas pricing policy provides a framework for establishing the minimum gas price that any category of gas buyer is charged. The policy is to ensure that gas is supplied at affordable and economic prices to different sectors of the domestic market. Each of these sectors has different price regime and structure. End user prices in the Nigerian domestic gas market have typically been set at levels below international gas prices. These low prices have provided limited commercial incentive for the primary resource holders in Nigeria to develop and produce gas for the domestic market. Gas producers have either decided to flare the gas or sell to the LNG plant since the commercial benefits from LNG sales have been more attractive.

The gas pricing policy objective is predicated on the development of a fully liberalized market. The conditions for a fully liberalized market do not currently exist as existing domestic gas prices are sub-commercial and inadequate to support significant natural gas development and production on a commercial basis. It is therefore the primary objective of this policy to increase gas prices for all potential suppliers to a level which will provide adequate commercial returns and stimulate development and growth in gas supply.

The transitional pricing policy[55] aims to transit from the existing sub-commercial pricing to market-led pricing depending on the development of a fully open market environment. The transitional pricing policy for natural gas will gradually move from the current low prices towards the export parity price, that is, the price currently

---

[54] Supra, see note 51
[55] Supra, see note 51

being achieved by suppliers to LNG facilities. Under these conditions, it is assumed that suppliers will be indifferent as to where the gas is supplied since the price will effectively be the same. The transitional pricing policy is a sector based gas pricing arrangement which breaks the domestic market into 3 (three) distinct sectors during the transition – power, gas based industries; and wholesale/local distribution companies. Pricing for each sector during the transition is developed to meet the specific objective for that sector and recognizes the specific challenges of each. Gas prices to the power sector have transitioned progressively from sub-commercial levels to $2.00 US dollars per million cubic feet (mcf) by 2014. The current gas price for the power sector has been increased to $2.50 US dollars per mcf and $0.80 cents per mcf for transportation costs.[56]

c. The Strategic Gas Aggregator

The NGMP requires the establishment of a Strategic Aggregator. The Gas Aggregation Company Nigeria Limited (GACN) was incorporated in Nigeria on 5th January 2010, by NNPC, Pan Ocean Oil Corporation (Nigeria) Limited, Chevron Nigeria, SPDC, Exxon Mobil and Total. The GACN is a non-profit making company that acts as the gas aggregator to manage the domestic supply obligations of gas producers, acts as interface between domestic buyers and upstream gas suppliers and oversees the overall network/system administration. The demand management role of the GACN will continue until the end of government's intervention through the DSO. The computation of aggregate price and management of the escrow account will continue until the expiration of the foundation Gas Sales and Purchase Agreements (GSPAs).

---

[56] The Presidential Task Force on Power, 'Gas Price Increase Will Boost Electricity Supply' http://nigeriapowerreform.org/index.php?option=com_content&view=article&id =1730:gas-price-increase-will-boost-electricity-supply-says-nerc&catid=36:sector-news&Itemid=336 last accessed on 8th April, 2015

d. The Partial Risk Guarantee

The World Bank Partial Risk Guarantee (PRG) will be issued to address issues of non-payment in the Nigerian gas market. The World Bank Partial Risk Guarantee is a revenue securitization scheme in case of default on payments. Gas producers and suppliers were reluctant to explore for and produce more gas for the domestic gas market dominated by power generation stations because of default in payment by the now defunct PHCN. According to the World Bank, the absence of long-term gas supply arrangements has affected the gas and power sectors adversely as gas had to be procured on a 'best endeavour' basis.[57]

The PRG is provided under the Nigeria Electricity and Gas Improvement Project (NEGIP) to enable long-term gas supply arrangements. Under the NEGIP, the World Bank has committed to a series of PRGs for a total of $400 million US dollars. In April 2013, the World Bank provided its first PRG for $145 million US dollars for the 10-year Gas Supply and Aggregation Agreement (GSAA) for the supply of gas to the Egbin power station. The arrangement allows Chevron Nigeria Ltd to supply gas to the Egbin power station. This was the first time that the Egbin power station will be able to procure gas under long-term arrangements.[58] With the PRG in place, more long term gas supply arrangements for the domestic gas sector will be concluded between power generating companies and gas producers and suppliers.

c. The Network Code[59]

The National Gas Transportation Network Code is intended to manage open access to the network, and is predicated on aspects of the United Kingdom network code. Essentially, the Network Code is intended to be a contractual framework between transporters and gas network users that provide open competitive access to existing and future gas transportation infrastructure. To support the successful

---

[57] World Bank, 'World Bank to help Nigeria Improve Gas Supply and Bring More Electricity to Nigerian Consumers' Press Release, April 2013 http://www.worldbank.org/en/news/press-release/2013/04/22/world-bank-to-help-nigeria-improve-gas-supply-and-reliability-and-bring-more-electricity-to-nigerian-consumers last accessed 8th April, 2015

[58] ibid

[59] Supra, see note 51

transportation of gas for power generation and other domestic use, the following key elements are included in the code:

- Gas entry requirements – this is particularly relevant to issues such as gas quality and the measurement and allocations of gas in order to ensure an appropriately consistent and equitable treatment;
- Transportation charges – this comprises capacity charges, commodity charges and overrun charges under the code. The applicable rates are set through publication of a statement published by the operator from time to time in accordance with a process overseen by the Department of Petroleum Resources (DPR);
- Metering and measurements – The provision and technical specification of measurement and metering stations;
- Nominations – The provision of nominations by shippers is designed to assist the Operator in managing the system.

f. The Gas Infrastructure Blueprint[60]

The development of gas infrastructure in Nigeria has largely been driven by field to plant connections with little or no consideration of the potential for an interconnected system. Despite this challenge, there have been some major segments of gas infrastructure developed over the years and as such a relatively robust interconnected pipeline network could be achieved with some key infrastructure additions connecting existing systems. There are few commercial incentives for private companies to become actively involved in the development and operation of gas infrastructure. A clear investment opportunity must be presented to potential developers for the desired gas grid to be established. The key objective of the gas infrastructure policy is to establish a clear opportunity for potential investors that will:

- Maximize the penetration and reach of natural gas across the country;
- Facilitate efficient connection of as many suppliers to as many demand centres in an integrated hub and dispatch structure;

---

[60] Supra, see note 51

- Where possible, leverage connectivity between domestic and export infrastructure for flexibility of supply;
- Provide for an efficient system to maximize the extraction of NGLs and other valuable by-products from the rich gas through the use of central processing facilities (CPFs).

The gas infrastructure policy is predicated on long run commerciality to support Public Private Partnership (PPP) and ultimately private sector investment. The infrastructure policy framework therefore focuses on back bone gas pipeline infrastructure and Central Processing Facilities (CPF) strategically located at designated hubs in the network. The pipelines are based on commercial principles of operation and access is governed by the national Network Code. The philosophy behind the blueprint is that feed gas from the flow stations and designated nodes of the upstream suppliers within a franchise area will be transported to a CPF, where gas will be treated and Natural Gas Liquids (NGL) extracted. The pipeline sales gas will then be evacuated through the nearest gas transmission pipeline system, whilst the extracted NGLs will be stored in NGL storage and handling facilities pending export into the domestic market or external markets.

The proposed CPFs are situated in three regions – the Western region, the Central region and the South Eastern region. There is a proposed network of three gas transmission pipeline systems[61]:

- **South-North Gas Transmission Pipeline System** – This planned pipeline will originate from the South Eastern region CPF, crossing through the Eastern states of Abia, Ebonyi, and Enugu to Kano and Kaduna via Ajaokuta and Abuja. This will be the main back bone system transmitting gas to the Eastern, Central, and Northern parts of Nigeria.

- **Western Gas Transmission System** – This pipeline comprises the existing Escravos-Lagos Pipeline System (ELPS), a planned offshore bypass originating from the Western region CPF linking up with the ELPS in Sagamu and

---

[61] Supra, see note 51

with provisions for a spur extension to the Olokola LNG plant. The system also includes a Western extension to Jebba, Kwara State and Osun State. It will serve the entire western region of Nigeria and enhance the capacity of ELPS.

- **Interconnector Gas Transmission System** – This pipeline will originate from the Central region CPF and comprise of a new pipeline to Oben as well as the existing Oben-Ajaokuta link. It will serve as an interconnector between the reserves rich Eastern area and the major Western and North-South Transmission Systems. It will provide access to additional gas supplies from the Eastern area to serve the market intensive West and North axis. In essence, this system will bridge the East, West and Northern parts of Nigeria with respect to gas access.

CHAPTER FOUR

LEGAL FRAMEWORK FOR ENERGY SECURITY IN NIGERIA's GAS SECTOR

This chapter discusses the existing gas related laws and regulations in Nigeria. The legal framework for energy security in Nigeria's gas sector is not robust. It is this weakness in legislation that the draft Petroleum Industry Bill, 2012, seeks to remedy. Currently, international protocols on gas, the Associated Gas Re-injection Act, 1979 (as amended), the Nigeria Liquefied Natural Gas Act, 1989 and the National Domestic Gas Supply and Price Regulations 2008 are the only legislations directed at the gas sector. The Petroleum Industry Bill 2012 makes extensive provisions for gas undertakings including the sphere already covered by the Associated Gas Re-Injection Act and the National Domestic Gas Supply and Price Regulations 2008. The bill is however, yet to be enacted into law.

4.1   International conventions and Protocols

a. United Nations Framework Convention on Climate Change (UNFCCC) 1992

The United Nations Framework Convention on Climate Change (UNFCCC) was the first global effort to address the problem of climate change caused by greenhouse gases. This framework was adopted in 1992 under the Earth Summit of the United Nations Conference on Environment and Development (UNCED) in Rio de Janeiro, Brazil, and came into force in 1992.[62] The Convention aimed to gather and share information on greenhouse gas emissions, national policies and best practices; to launch national strategies to tackle greenhouse gases emissions, financial support and technology transfer for developing countries; and preparation for adaptation to climate change. This convention envisaged stabilising greenhouse emissions to the levels that would prevent dangerous interference with the climate system[63]. Nigeria became signatory to the Convention on 13th June, 1992. On August 29, 1994, Nigeria ratified its commitments to the convention but is yet to domesticate the Convention. The Climate Change Commission Bill, which seeks to domesticate the Convention is still pending before the national legislature.

b. Global Gas Flaring Reduction Initiative (GGFR)

The Global Gas Flaring Reduction (GGFR) is a World Bank public-private partnership initiative which was launched during the World Summit on Sustainable Development in Johannesburg, South Africa in 2002. This partnership which is led by World Bank, includes gas producing countries, major gas companies and international organisations involved in oil and gas business. This partnership has the mandate to catalyse the reduction of gases that would otherwise be flared through policy change, stakeholders' facilitation, projects implementation and the supports of oil producing nations and companies to increasing the use of associated gases. The partnership also envisages promoting effective regulatory frameworks, and tackling gas utilisation constrains such as poor access to local and

---

[62] See Article 23 of the United Nations Framework Convention on Climate Change (UNFCCC) 1992
[63] Article 2, UNFCCC, 1992

international markets, insufficient infrastructure particularly in developing countries like Nigeria. Nigeria, through her National petroleum corporation (NNPC) is a partner to this initiative.

The GGFR provides opportunity for all stakeholders to discuss ways to address the disastrous effects of gas flaring and seize the economic, financial and environmental opportunities associated to gas utilization. The GGFR encourages cooperation on awareness, technology dissemination, policy dialogue and regulation development to tackle gas flaring. The World Bank advocates that before gas flaring is adopted, feasible alternatives for the use of the gas should be evaluated and integrated into production design to the maximum extent possible[64]. Flaring volumes for new facilities should be estimated during the initial commissioning period so that fixed volume flaring targets can be developed.

GGFR realizes that gas flaring reduction requires political, social and economic will that requires good management framework to effectively manage and utilize gas resources to achieve economic goals. Another challenge identified by the GGFR is that many oil producing nations tend to have operational weakness in their monitoring, compliance and enforcement institutions to effectively monitor gas flaring. The GGFR has also identified that apart from putting in place investment in gas utilisation projects and incentives for gas production, good gas pricing policy is necessary for gas reduction programmes. The GGFR encourages a regime of gas pricing that meets the need of all stakeholders.

The World Bank Group's standard practice is that the volumes of gas flared for all flaring events should be accurately recorded and reported. This approach is based on the understanding that scientific knowledge is imperative for formulating, designing and implementing gas flaring reduction programmes. Where relevant data is not readily available, reliable or sufficient there will be problem in ensuring effective implementation of policies.[65]

---

[64] See International Finance Corporation 'Environmental, Health, and Safety Guidelines for onshore oil and gas development' 2007

[65] Suma Chakrabarti, speech delivered at the GGFR Partnership Forum, London, 24th October 2012. http://www.ebrd.com/news/2012/speech-transcript-suma-

4.2   Nigerian legislation

a. Associated Gas Re-Injection Act 1979

The Associated Gas Re-Injection Act seeks to compel gas pricing companies in Nigeria to submit preliminary programmes and detailed plans for implementation of gas re-injection to the Minister for Petroleum Resources. This includes projects and schemes to utilize or re-inject all gas produced in association with oil. The Act prohibits flaring of associated gas without the consent of the Minister for Petroleum Resources.[66] The Minister can also permit the continued flaring of associated gas if he is satisfied that the utilization or re-injection of the associated gas is not feasible.[67] The challenge with this provision is the subjective discretionary powers given to the Minister to determine whether utilization or re-injection is feasible or not. This anomaly was addressed in the Associated Gas Re-Injection (Continued Flaring of Gas) Regulations 1985. The Regulations specified the following conditions for issuance of Certificate for continued flaring or gas:

- Where more than 75 percent of the gas produced is effectively utilized or conserved;
- Where the produced gas contains more than 15 percent impurities which render the gas unsuitable for industrial purposes;
- Where an on-going utilization programme is interrupted by equipment failure provided the period of interruption is not more than 3 months;
- Where the Minister in appropriate cases as he may deem fit, orders the production of oil from a field that does not satisfy any of the conditions specified in the Regulations.

Gas producers who flare gas without the consent of the Minister are liable to forfeit their concessions or leases. In practice this penalty is rarely imposed on defaulters.

---

chakrabarti-at-the-global-gas-flaring-reduction-ggfr-partnership-forum-on-24-october-2012-in-london-.html last accessed April 11, 2015.

[66] Section 3, Associated Gas Re-Injection Act, 1979
[67] ibid

Although the Act imposed obligation on gas producers to develop and initiate gas utilization projects, it was the Nigerian government that initiated most of the gas utilization projects that have led to a drastic reduction of flared gas. The gas producers were always in the habit of making excuses why they have to continue flaring gas. Without government intervention in initiating gas utilization projects, the Associated Gas Re-injection Act would have had very little or no significance at all.

b. Nigeria Liquefied Natural Gas (fiscal incentives, guarantees and assurances) Act 1989

The Nigeria Liquefied Natural Gas (fiscal incentives, guarantees and assurances) Act 1989, conferred pioneer status on the NLNG Limited and granted a tax relief period of 10 (ten) years to the NLNG Limited beginning from the date of the first commercial delivery of liquefied gas produced by the company.[68] This implies that the NLNG Limited between October 9, 1999, when it delivered its first cargo to and October 8, 2009, it did not pay tax.

The NLNG Limited was also exempted from payment of customs duties and all other duties, levies and charges.[69] The NLNG Limited was also allowed to deduct interest payable on loans for tax purposes, including interests on loans which accrued during the tax relief period.[70] This implies that between 1989 when the NLNG Limited was incorporated and October 2009, when its tax relief period elapsed, all accrued interests on loans obtained for its developmental projects were deducted for tax purposes. These incentives encouraged the NLNG to invest in LNG facilities and LNG export has proven to be a major breakthrough for Nigeria's gas industry. Nigeria is benefitting immensely from the development of LNG export business. Nigeria requires more tailor-made incentives codified into legislation for different sub-sectors of the gas industry in the quest for energy security in the gas sector.

---

[68] Section 2, Nigeria Liquefied Natural Gas Act, 1989
[69] Section 7, Nigeria Liquefied Natural Gas Act, 1989
[70] Section 5, Nigeria Liquefied Natural Gas Act, 1989

c. National Domestic Gas Supply and Price Regulations 2008

The National Domestic Gas Supply and Pricing Regulations 2008, established the Department of Gas empowered to announce the annual domestic demand requirement.[71] The domestic gas demand requirement is the aggregate of the quantity of gas required to meet the gas demand for strategic sectors within the domestic economy for a specific period of time.[72] The Department of Gas is also empowered to maintain surveillance over indices relevant to gas pricing, identifying macro-economic factors with relation to the price of gas and advice the Nigerian government on appropriate strategies. The Department of Gas also allocates the Domestic Gas Supply Obligation to every producer of petroleum and sets the aggregate price used by the gas aggregator.[73] Regulation 3 of the Regulations provides that the Department of Gas shall collaborate with suppliers of gas to establish a domestic gas aggregator to monitor the demand and supply of gas in the domestic market and act as intermediary between suppliers and purchasers of gas. The Gas Aggregation Company of Nigeria (GACN) was established in 2010 pursuant to this regulation.

Gas producers are required to submit a gas production and supply plan consistent with its obligations under the domestic gas demand requirement to the Department of Gas. Gas producers are also required to supply gas to purchasers in accordance with a gas purchase order issued by the aggregator. Gas producers are also required to pay compensation to purchasers for any losses suffered as a result of default to supply gas in compliance with the order of the gas aggregator.[74] Regulation 6[75] prescribes penalties for non compliance with gas supply obligations imposed on gas producers. Gas producers are required to pay for the volumes not supplied, based on the take or pay provisions of the executed Gas Sales and Purchase Agreement or $3.50 US dollars per Mscf, whichever is

---

[71] Regulation 2(a) National Domestic Gas Supply and Pricing Regulations 2008

[72] See Regulation 9, National Domestic Gas Supply and Pricing Regulations 2008

[73] Regulation 2(d) & (e) National Domestic Gas Supply and Pricing Regulations 2008. This function will be performed by the Downstream Petroleum Regulatory Agency (DPRA) when the PIB is enacted into law.

[74] Regulation 5 National Domestic Gas Supply and Pricing Regulations 2008

[75] ibid

higher. The Minister for Petroleum is also empowered to review this penalty whenever the Minister deemed fit. Gas producers who defaulted in their gas supply obligation would also be prevented from supplying gas to any export project in addition to any other penalty that the Minister may deem fit to impose.

4.3   The Gas Provisions of the Petroleum Industry Bill 2012

The major challenge with the draft Petroleum Industry Bill 2012 as it affects energy security in Nigeria is with regards to the bill's fiscal provisions that increase the tax obligations of gas investors especially in the upstream. It would have been expected that having witnessed the success of the NLNG Limited due partly to the fiscal incentives granted under the Nigeria LNG Act, 1989, the Nigerian government would have adopted the same method of incentivizing upstream gas activities in order to attract investment into gas exploration and development. The converse is however the case with the Petroleum Industry Bill. Rather than incentivizing upstream gas activities, the bill has increased tax obligations for upstream gas activities. This would not advance Nigeria's quest for energy security in gas production and supply. Rather, the fiscal provisions of the bill have the potential of discouraging investors from investing in the upstream gas activities, which Nigeria needs if energy security in gas will be achieved.

The draft Petroleum Industry Bill (PIB) 2012 has the potential to enable Nigeria attain energy security in both the domestic and export gas markets. The licensing of downstream gas activities will provide the clarity investors need to determine the market segment in which they want to invest and be involved. Regulations dealing with anti-competitive behavior, abuse of market power and consumer protection by stakeholders in the domestic gas market will also create conducive environment for investors to participate in the domestic gas market. The provisions on pricing and tariff also have the potential to stimulate investments in the domestic gas sector due to the systematic transition from regulated prices to prices determined by market forces. Transition from regulated to market-driven prices within a specific timeline is incentive to investors that they will be able to recoup their huge investments in gas undertakings.

a. Downstream Gas Licences Under the PIB

The draft Petroleum Industry Bill (PIB) 2012 is designed to support gas supply and utilization in Nigeria's domestic gas market. The bill therefore makes provisions for licensing downstream gas activities[76]. The Downstream Petroleum Regulatory Agency (DPRA) is empowered to grant downstream licences for

- Constructing and operating process plant, including those for gas liquefaction;
- Constructing and operating gas transportation pipelines;
- Constructing and operating gas transportation networks;
- Constructing and operating gas distribution networks;
- Undertaking the supply of downstream natural gas; or
- Owning and running downstream natural gas processing or retail facility.

Part V(B) of the bill provides specifically for 4 (four) separate downstream gas licences. These are the transportation pipeline owner licence, transportation network operator licence, gas supply licence, and gas distribution licence. The duties and obligations imposed on holders of these licences are geared towards ensuring security of gas supply to the domestic gas market.

Transportation Pipeline Owner Licence(TPOL) -A gas transportation pipeline owner may be granted the 3 separate rights to own, operate and maintain a gas transportation pipeline within a defined route.[77] The owner of a gas transportation pipeline is prevented from doing

---

[76] Section 206 of the PIB generally provides that the Downstream Petroleum Regulatory Agency (DPRA) shall have power to grant downstream licences. These licences relate generally to undertakings in oil, gas or condensates. Without such licences, no person shall conduct any downstream petroleum operations. Section 206 makes reference generally to petroleum, downstream petroleum operations and petroleum products. The definition of these terms in section 362, however, includes gas products and gas related undertakings.
[77] Section 230 of the PIB

anything which in the opinion of the DPRA prevents, restricts or distorts competition.[78]

Transportation Network Operator Licence (TNOL) - The gas transportation network operator controls the conveyance of gas from high pressured terminals to the distributors and wholesalers. This is achieved through a network of gas transportation pipelines owned and maintained by the transportation pipeline owners. The transportation network operator is therefore likely to enter into separate contractual relationships with the transportation pipeline owners, gas distributors and wholesalers.

A gas transportation network operator is empowered by the bill to conduct certain activities. These include the conveyance of gas through transportation network and balancing inputs and off takes from the transportation network. The activities also includes providing third party access to the transportation network and charging appropriate tariffs for the use of the transportation network.[79]

The bill also imposes certain duties on the transport network operator. The duties include ensuring an equitable and transparent access to the transportation network, establishing and publishing terms and conditions for access to the network, developing a network code for the operator's own network in line with the general guidelines for network code by issued by the DPRA, and entering into contracts with gas transportation pipeline owners, gas distributors and wholesale customers for connection to and operation of the transportation network.[80]

Gas Supply Licence (GSL) - By section 237 of the bill a Gas Supply Licence (GSL) is required to supply gas to the downstream gas sector. A producer of gas intending to supply gas into the downstream sector shall be a qualified person entitled to apply for

---

[78] Section 231 of the PIB
[79] Section 233 of the PIB
[80] Section 234 of the PIB

and be issued a GSL. It is not clear whether only gas producers are qualified for the GSL. It is however clear that it is mandatory to grant the GSL to gas producers, if and whenever they decide to apply for it.

A gas supplier has a duty to ensure that there is reliable supply of gas in an economically feasible manner. There is also a duty to do nothing, which in the opinion of the DPRA may prevent, restrict or distort competition.[81] This provision seeks to guarantee security in supply of gas to the domestic market.

The holder of a GSL has the right to supply, sell and deliver gas to purchasers anywhere in Nigeria. Section 239 of the bill provides for specific rights of the gas supplier. It is advisable that parties include terms reflecting such rights in their GSPAs. The reason is that section 239(2) of the bill makes the sale of gas by suppliers to wholesale customers subject to the provisions of the bill. The supplier has the following rights:

- The right to terminate supply to a customer in the event of non-payment. The notice period and disconnection procedure in the event of termination are subject to regulations to be made by the DPRA.
- The right to recover from the customer all costs reasonably incurred in the supply of gas. This right is however subject to any restrictions or conditions imposed by the DPRA with respect to the level and structure of the charges.
- The right to enter any premises to remove, read, test or disconnect meters. This right is however to be undertaken in accordance with a metering code to be issued by the DPRA.

Gas Distribution Licence (GDL) - A Gas Distribution Licence (GDL) confers the exclusive right to own and operate a gas distribution system and to distribute gas within a local distribution zone to customers that are not wholesale customers.[82] The GDL

---

[81] Section 238 of the PIB

confers on the gas distributor the right to own pipelines since the gas distributor would need to develop a network of distribution pipelines. The GDL also confers exclusive network operation rights on the gas distributor to operate the distribution network.

The bill imposes some conditions on the gas distributor to ensure that it connects the customers within its local distribution zone in the manner laid out by DPRA.[83] The gas distributors shall also conduct its activities in accordance with safe environmental standards and comply with consumer protection measures set out in the bill.

The bill makes provision for certain obligations of the gas distributor.[84] The obligations include but are not limited to the following:

- Developing and operating an economical distribution network for the safe, reliable and efficient distribution of gas on request to any customer and connect all customers within its local distribution zone.

- Cooperate with the DPRA to develop the Network Code for the gas distribution system. The Network code is to guide the operations of gas distribution. The Network Code that there is an adequate supply within the distribution zone according to the identified demand.

- Subject to safety and network capacity constraints, to distribute gas on request to any customer capable of paying for connection to the distribution network.

- Do nothing to prevent, restrict or distort competition. This duty is however not to distort competition is not relevant since the licence is exclusive.

The gas distributor has rights similar to those of the gas supplier.[85]

---

[82] Section 241 of the PIB
[83] Section 244 of the PIB
[84] Section 242 of the PIB
[85] Section 243 of the PIB

These rights are subject to the restrictions and conditions imposed by the DPRA with respect to the level and structure of the distributor's charges. The gas distributor can enter premises of a customer to read meters and test equipment, recover on the basis of an invoice, costs reasonably incurred in the provision of the appropriate infrastructure.

b. Competition and market regulation

The provisions of the bill as regards competition are mainly focused on the downstream gas sector. Generally, competition law provides safeguards for consumer welfare and free and open markets to all market participants. This is achieved by provisions, which encourage the free flow of products and services at the lowest prices; provisions on merger control and dominance, abuse of market power, product quality and availability issues. The bill provides generally against unfair conditions for supply of products or provision of service, contracts, arrangements, collaborations or understanding intended to manipulate market prices, conducting activities for the purpose of market sharing, permitting, influencing or imposing embargoes or boycotts on a competitor and engaging in any other conduct which the DPRA deems anti-competitive.[86]

Obligation To Avoid Anti-Competitive Behaviour - The bill imposes specific obligation on gas pipeline owners, gas suppliers and gas distributors not to do anything to prevent, restrict or distort competition.[87] There is no such specific obligation on the gas transportation network operator. There is, however, a general obligation not to restrict or prevent competition imposed on all licencees in section 262 of the bill.

Market Dominance - The provisions of the bill regarding market dominance only relate to the DPRA's power to regulate prices and impose sanctions where dominant position is abused. There is no clear provision prohibiting market dominance. There is also no provision regarding dominance threshold to determine what constitutes market dominance. Where the Minister on the advice of

---

[86] Section 262 of the PIB
[87] Sections 231(1)(e), 238(1)(b) and 242(i) of the PIB

the DPRA determines that a particular licenced activity is a monopoly or a particular licencee is a dominant provider, and competition has not developed to protect gas customers, the DPRA shall have power to regulate the prices.[88] Before undertaking a price review or methodology, the DPRA shall consult with licencees, industry participants and stakeholders.

Dealing With Anti-Competitive Behaviour And Abuse of Market Power - Sections 257 and 263 of the bill provides extensively for the powers of the DPRA to determine and impose sanctions for anti-competitive behaviour and abuse of market power in the downstream gas sector. The DPRA's power to determine, pronounce upon, administer, monitor and enforce compliance of anti-competitive behaviour is exclusive. What constitutes abuse of market power is however not clearly defined[89]. Violation of fair hearing rules would certainly be a major concern regarding the exclusive administrative, investigative, quasi-judicial and enforcement powers of the DPRA. Where in the opinion of the DPRA, there is or may be, or exists a likelihood of anti-competitive behaviour and abuse of market power, the DPRA is given investigative, quasi-judicial and enforcement powers to deal with such matters. In this regard, the DPRA may undertake inquiries and investigations, require and compel the disclosure of information from such licencees, issue cease and desist orders, levy fines which shall be set out in regulations issued pursuant to the bill from time to time, make pronouncements/findings on its investigations, and monitor and enforce compliance with the

---

[88] Section 252 of the PIB

[89] This is unlike the Singapore Gas Act 2001, which defines conduct that constitutes abuse of dominant position. Section 70(2) of the Singapore Gas Act provides that conduct may in particular, constitute such an abuse if it consists in – (a) Directly or indirectly imposing unfair purchase or selling prices or other unfair trading conditions of gas (b) Limiting production, markets or technical developments in the gas industry in Singapore to the prejudice of customers (c) Applying dissimilar conditions to equivalent transactions with other trading parties, thereby placing them at a competitive disadvantage (d) Making the conclusion of contracts subject to acceptance by the other parties of supplementary obligations which, by their nature or according to commercial usage, have no connection with the subject of the contracts.

provisions of the bill relating to anti-competition and with any competition laws and regulations.

The DPRA is saddled with the responsibility to monitor the state of the gas market so as to determine whether there is any anti-competitive activity being carried on. Where in the opinion of the DPRA, there has been an abuse or threatened abuse of market power, the DPRA may serve and publish a notice on such company. The notice shall specify the abuse or threatened abuse, and the intention of the DPRA to issue a cease and desist order. The notice shall also specify the remedy and timescale. Where the company fails to comply, the DPRA may issue a cease and desist order. Failure to comply with a cease and desist order shall be an offence punishable by a fine of ₦50,000,000.00 (Fifty Million Naira) and a revocation of the relevant licence.[90]

Neither a cease and desist order nor a fine can be issued or imposed in two situations. Firstly, if a company involved demonstrates to the satisfaction of the DPRA that it has not abused or is not threatening to abuse its market power. Secondly, a cease and desist order or a fine may also not be issued or imposed if the company involved has ceased to abuse or ceased from the threat to abuse its market power. This second instance is capable of eroding the essence of such cease and desist order. The reason is that there would be no deterrent in the form of a fine or compensation required from companies who have engaged in and completed the acts complained of. This concern is however allayed by section 264(9) of the bill. Where a person has ceased to abuse or has ceased from the threat to abuse its market power, the DPRA may impose an appropriate penalty on one condition. That is, if it is found that such threat or threat of abuse was deliberate.

Gaps in the PIB regarding Anti-Trust - The anti-trust provisions of the bill have no clear provision prohibiting market dominance. There is also no provision regarding dominance threshold to determine

---

[90] Section 264 of the PIB

what constitutes market dominance. The determination of dominance threshold is left to the discretion of the DPRA. What constitutes abuse of market power or dominant position is not clearly defined and is also left to the discretion of the DPRA.

Section 258 of the bill provides that in order to protect the interests of gas customers, the DPRA may advise the Minister to issue consumer protection regulations. This duty to advise the Minister on the issuance of consumer protection regulations is left to the discretion of the DPRA. There is also no specific time frame after the bill is enacted within which such regulations are to be made. These shortfalls may have the effect of defeating the essence of the consumer protection provision in the bill.

In cases of an emergency, the bill gives the DPRA the discretion to designate distributors and suppliers of last resort to provide services to customers.[91] This provision is necessary because the gas distributor has exclusive rights within the local distribution zone. The absence of such a provision would leave customers without options and exposed to exploitation. The provision is applicable in three situations. Firstly, where an existing distributor for a local distribution zone or a supplier becomes insolvent, or has its licences suspended or revoked. Secondly, in the event that the distributor for a local distribution zone or supplier refuses or fails to fulfill the terms of its licence to distribute or supply gas to customers. Thirdly, in such other circumstances as determined by the DPRA. A major concern with the third condition is that the exclusive distribution rights of the gas distributor may be undermined without prior clearly stated conditions.

c. Third Party Access Rights

Third Party Access (TPA) right to pipelines is key in ensuring security of supply in the domestic gas market. TPA provides guarantee to end users and sellers for the delivery of gas. The bill provides considerably for third party access rights with some safeguards for the rights of gas pipeline owners, gas suppliers and distributors. The efficacy of such provisions may be undermined by the absence of

---

[91] Section 259 of the PIB

unbundling obligations of gas undertakings. A vertically integrated gas company with pipeline ownership, supply and distribution undertakings will still be in a better position compared to third parties. The Nigerian gas market is characterized by two major economic and structural aspects. Firstly, the NGC currently has monopoly in pipeline transportation of gas. The required gas transportation infrastructure is capital intensive. Duplication of this infrastructure may also be undesirable from an environmental perspective. The second aspect is that transportation of gas is integrated into gas sales activities. Companies need to transport gas to their customers through pipelines. Control over the pipeline facilities is therefore crucial.

TPA is a key instrument by which the bill intends to increase competition in the Nigerian gas market. Gas suppliers and customers are given the right to have their gas transported through pipelines that they do not own or control. Suppliers can therefore sell gas directly to customers to which they are not connected. This will lead to market expansion for each gas supplier and increased competition among suppliers. The pipeline owner's supply division is however, exposed to competition. From the customer's perspective, TPA establishes a right to choose the supplier of gas.

The General Network Code - The TPA system in the bill is based on regulated conditions rather than negotiation by the parties involved. The DPRA is empowered to establish guidelines for a general Network Code for the transportation and distribution networks of the downstream gas industry.[92] The bill also provides for each pipeline owner and network operator to have specific network codes which comply with the general Network Code. The DPRA develops the guidelines in consultation with licencees and other stakeholders. The guidelines are to include the following;

- A connection policy, standard terms for connection to the transportation and distribution network as well as the charging methodology,
- A mechanism by which users reserve capacity in the transportation network or distribution network,

---

[92] Sections 246(1) and 249(2) of the PIB

- A mechanism for allocating capacity between users in the event that at any time there is a greater demand for access than there is available capacity.

The general Network Code allows for TPA to a transportation pipeline, transportation network or a distribution network. These can be for the purpose of transportation of gas to points of consumption, subject to compliance with the prescribed conditions of the network code of the pipeline. By section 249 of the bill, a person shall be permitted access to a transportation pipeline, a transportation network or a distribution network for the purpose of having gas transported to points of consumption. The access is subject to compliance with prescribed terms and conditions for access stated in the Network Code of the particular pipeline.

Regulated Open Access Facilities - The DPRA may designate gas pipelines and other facilities currently owned by downstream operators as 'regulated open access facilities'. Any licenced company may be permitted access to such facilities.[93]

TPA Obligations of Downstream Gas Operators - The transportation pipeline owner has the following TPA obligations under the bill[94]:

- Manage supply shortfalls and where feasible, meet requests of customers for transportation above contractual volumes.
- Provides third party access to the transportation network.
- Ensure equitable and transparent access to the transportation network;
- Establish and publish terms and conditions for access to the network;
- Enter into agreements with transportation pipeline owners, distributors, and where appropriate, wholesale customers, for connection to and operation of the transportation network;
- Develop the network code for its own network in line with guidelines for the general network code by the Agency.

---

[93] Section 222 of the PIB
[94] Section 231(1)(b), 233(1)(c), 234(1)(c – f) and 240(c) of the PIB

- Supply gas on request to a customer capable of paying for connection to the gas transportation network, subject to safety and network capacity constraints.

The transportation pipeline owner has the following TPA obligations in the bill[95]:

- distribute gas on request to any customer capable of paying for connection to the distribution network, subject to safety and network capacity constraints;
- Connect all customers within its local distribution zone in accordance with prescribed regulations if it is economically practicable to do so;
- Publish terms and conditions of access to its distribution network as required.

<u>Conditions for Third Party Access</u> - Access to the gas transportation network and gas distribution network shall be on:

- A non-discriminatory basis between system users with similar characteristics
- In respect of any available capacity, provided that such capacity is not subject to a previous contractual commitment
- In accordance with and governed by the terms and conditions of the network codes approved by the DPRA.[96]

Accordingly, connection agreements may be entered into between:

a.   A gas customer and a gas distributor
b.   A gas transportation pipeline owner and a gas transportation network operator
c.   A distributor and the transportation network operator, when a gas distribution network connects to the main gas transportation network
d.   A supplier and a transportation pipeline owner or transportation network operator.

---

[95] Section 242 of the PIB
[96] Section 250 of the PIB

<u>Equality and Non-Discrimination In Allocating Available Pipeline Capacity</u> - The core of TPA is the duty of the pipeline owner to transport gas as long as there are unused pipeline volumes. Access must be given on equal terms and conditions for all system users, including the related undertakings of the pipeline owner. Section 250 of the bill provides that access to the gas transportation network and gas distribution network shall be on a non-discriminatory basis between system users with similar characteristics[97]. Similarly, Section 234(1)(c-f) of the bill requires the transportation network operator to ensure equitable and transparent access to the transportation network. The guidelines for the general Network Code suggest that where available capacity are inadequate, such capacity would be allocated in a way that every user gets a fair share of access. The implication of this is that some users may have to reduce their contracted volumes in such situations.

TPA implies that some of the customers of the pipeline company have the option to switch their gas supplier, while still using the same pipeline company as transporter. The bill requires the pipeline owner to treat his own supply or distribution branch and other suppliers and distributors equally. This implies that the pipeline owner must compete for scarce capacity. For several reasons, total non-discrimination between the owner and third parties can be difficult. The pipeline owner may legitimately have preferential access to scarce capacity. The bill does not prevent a single entity from owning and operating gas transportation pipelines while at the same time engaging in gas supply and distribution. There is neither a duty of unbundling nor is there a duty to organise separate legal entities. By controlling the desirable infrastructure, the pipeline owner has incentives to protect his own gas supply activities from competition.

Increased pipeline capacity is important in ensuring the Nigerian government's objectives of security of supply and the transformation

---

[97] This is similar to Article 32(1) of the European Union Gas Directive 2009/73/EC applicable in the European Union, which provides for a system of third party access to the transmission and distribution system without discrimination between system users.

of the national gas markets into one single, interconnected market. It should also be noted that the bill makes provision for transport tariffs to cover investment costs on pipeline infrastructure. Section 254(2) of the bill provides that tariffs charged for the use of the gas transportation network shall reflect efficient investment and capital costs, efficient operating and maintenance expenses and a reasonable return to licencees on their investments. The bill therefore provides some incentives for investments in pipeline infrastructure without giving the owner priority to scarce capacity.

Reservation of Pipeline Capacity - The guidelines for the general Network Code suggest that users can reserve capacity. The bill is silent as to whether such reserved capacity right is tradable or liable to be forfeited on a use-it-or-lose-it basis so that they could be made available to other third party users. This would have been a more pro-competitive approach. Gas markets are usually characterized by long-term transportation and supply contracts, vertical integration and the danger of insufficient pipeline capacity. Large pipeline volumes are therefore, and will still for several years be bound by already committed volumes. Under these circumstances, there is a danger that reserved capacity volumes will be used, or abused, as a barrier to increased competition[98].

Refusal of Third Party Access - Inadequate capacity, safety concerns and economic reasons can make denial of pipeline access legitimate.

---

[98] In the US case of *American Central Eastern Texas Gas Co v Union Pacific Resources Group Inc* No 02-41010 (5th c 2004) the defendant company required its customers to enter into long-term agreements in order to fill its pipelines and thus excluding others attempting to enter the same market. The strategy was to employ a web of long-term agreements with existing customers in the market to prevent entry of third parties. Where some capacity existed and where potential new entrants sought access to the pipelines, the company made the access conditional on certain uneconomic charges. The company also refused to give guarantees over the capacity, thus making access unworkable in practice. This case was heard as an appeal from a decision by an arbitral tribunal. The arbitration award involved finding monopolization under *Section 2 of the Sherman Anti-Trust Act*. The arbitrator held that the company had violated the provision. The US Court of Appeals also affirmed the earlier decision of a District Court that had already confirmed the arbitration award.

By sections 240 and 242 of the bill, the obligation of gas suppliers and distributors to supply and distribute gas to a customer capable of paying for connection is subject to safety and network capacity constraints. Article 35(1) of the Gas Directive applicable in the European Union has similar conditions for refusal of access. Natural gas undertakings may refuse access to the system (1) on the basis of lack of capacity (2) where the access to the system would prevent them from carrying out the public service obligations assigned to them (3) on the basis of serious economic and financial difficulties with take-or-pay contracts. In the third instance, there is an obligation to make the necessary enhancements as far as it is economic to do so or when a potential customer is willing to pay for them. By article 48 of the Gas Directive, where a natural gas undertaking encounters, or considers it would encounter, serious economic and financial difficulties because of its take-or-pay commitments accepted in one or more gas-purchase contracts, it may send an application for a temporary derogation from Article 32 to the member state concerned or the designated competent authority. Where a natural gas undertaking has refused access, the application shall be presented without delay. The applications shall be accompanied by all relevant information on the nature and extent of the problem and on the efforts undertaken by the natural gas undertaking to solve the problem. Natural gas undertakings which have not been granted a derogation shall not refuse, or shall no longer refuse, access to the system because of take-or-pay commitments accepted in a gas purchase contract.

Objective Business Justification - A decision to refuse to deal with a specific company can be based on an objective and legitimate business justification. Refusal on this ground must however not be based on anti-competitive motive[99]. Section 250 of the bill which

---

[99] In the US, the use of long-term contracts to block entry was relevant in the *American Central Eastern Texas Gas Co v Union Pacific Resources Group Inc.* In that case, the defendant company had employed a strategy of excluding competitors. The company required its customers to enter into long-term agreements in order to fill its pipelines. This was capable of preventing third party access. In the case of *the City of Chanute, Kansas v Williams Natural Gas Co* 955 F.2d 641 (10 c 1992) eight cities claimed that the pipeline company had refused to transport gas purchased from third-party suppliers by the cities. The US Court of Appeals recognized the

provides that access right available for only capacity not subject to previous contractual commitment supports the argument for refusal of access on the basis of business justification. Section 242 of the bill, which provides that gas distributors connect customers if it is economically practicable to do so, also lends credence to the business justification argument. It is important to acknowledge that even a monopolist is free to choose its trading partners and can refuse a business relationship with a particular company.

d. Pricing and Tariff Methodology

The DPRA will oversee tariffs for gas transportation by pipelines, bulk storage of gas in depots designated as regulated open access facilities, and any regulated open access facility.[100]

---

monopoly that the pipeline company had in the cities. The appeal court however, held that there was a legitimate business explanation for the refusal of access. The pipeline company had the right to temporarily refuse TPA and related transportation services because of previous take-or-pay agreements that it had concluded. These agreements, under which the pipeline company had committed to purchase certain volumes of gas from producers, amounted to a significant value. In a similar case, *State of Illinois ex rel. Burris v. Panhandle Eastern Pipe Line Co* 935 F.2d 1469 (7th c 1991) the state claimed that Panhandle refused to transport through its pipelines, natural gas purchased its customers from third parties. Panhandle had contracted to purchase expensive gas through long-term take-or-pay agreements. When gas prices eventually dropped, the gas sold by Panhandle remained costly and its customers started to look for alternative sources. Panhandle, however, had a 'sole supplier' provision in the contracts with its customers. Panhandle also had an obligation to use its best efforts to meet customer demand for gas. Significantly, to satisfy this obligation, Panhandle entered into a number of long-term contracts to secure sufficient gas volumes for the future. When the customers of Panhandle requested the company to transport the gas they had purchased from third-party producers, Panhandle refused. The refusal was based on the ground that enabling its customers to obtain gas from other sources exposes the company to enormous take-or-pay liability. The District Court, affirmed by the Court of Appeal, looked at the issue from an essential facility angle. The court held that it would have been economically feasible for competitors to duplicate much of Panhandle's system within central Illinois by means of interconnections between competing pipelines and the construction of new pipelines. The Court also held that to be liable for monopolizing an essential facility it must be economically feasible for the owner of the facility to provide access to its facility. In this case the refusal was genuinely and reasonably motivated by the need to limit its potential take-or-pay liability, not by a desire to maintain its monopoly position by excluding competition in the sale of natural gas.

Tariff Methodology and Price Fixing - In establishing tariff methodologies, the DPRA shall take into account the existence of any subsidy given to the operators from which they directly benefit. The DPRA shall also consider favorable financing terms and any other matter that impacts directly or indirectly on tariff methodologies. The DPRA also has the power to establish tariff methodologies that reflect the terms and conditions of a contract between operators or between an operator and one or more eligible customers. Before a new price regime becomes effective the DPRA shall give notice in at least two national newspapers and on the DPRA's website; indicate period within which any aggrieved person may raise objections on the proposed methodology; and indicate the date of a public hearing during which the DPRA shall conduct for the discussion of the methodology.

Prior to the establishment of the tariff methodology, the DPRA shall

- consider any representations made by applicants, operators, consumers, prospective customers, consumers associations and persons reasonably expected
- obtain evidence, information or advice from any person possessing relevant expert knowledge

The DPRA shall thereafter fix a date on which tariff methodology becomes effective and shall publish the date in 2 national newspapers and on its website. The DPRA also has the liberty to change the tariff methodology if it believes it needs to be changed. The DPRA must however, conduct a public hearing before doing so.

Gas Pricing Principles - Section 252 of the bill, relating to gas pricing, provides that The DPRA shall have the power to regulate the prices charged or the revenues earned by the licensees where the Minister,

---

[100] Section 224 of the PIB

on advice of the DPRA determines that a particular licensed activity is a monopoly service, competition has not yet developed to such an extent as to protect the interests of customers or a particular licensee is a dominant provider. The DPRA in exercising its powers to regulate downstream gas prices shall be guided by the following principles:[101]

- prices shall be disaggregated into the component elements of the supply chain, including the costs of wholesale gas, transportation, distribution and supply
- prices shall reflect the costs incurred for the efficient provision of that activity
- prices charges shall permit a reasonable return for licenses on their investments
- prices shall not discriminate between customers with similar characteristics, similar size or similar consumption profile

Downstream gas licensees are entitled to propose and impose tariffs for approval by the DPRA before imposing the tariff on their customers.[102]

Tariffs for Gas Transport Arrangements - Tariffs charged for the use of the gas transportation network shall reflect, efficient investment and capital costs, efficient operating and maintenance expenses and reasonable return to licensees on their investments. Regulated customer prices shall reflect the transportation tariff, the reasonable costs incurred in the purchase of wholesale gas, reasonable return to the supplier, efficient supply charges covering billing, metering and other services relating to gas supply and the distribution tariff, if the customer is connected to a distribution network.

Wholesale Gas Prices - Section 255 of the bill provides that wholesale

---

[101] Section 253 of the PIB
[102] Section 254 of the PIB

gas supply between the holder of the GSL and the wholesale customer shall be negotiated directly between the parties on an arms' length basis. The gas transfer price between the upstream gas producer and a downstream gas purchaser shall reflect the costs of transfer between the parties. The DPRA shall have power to monitor wholesale gas supply transactions to ensure that the transfer price is undertaken on a transparent arm's length basis.

e. Domestic Gas Supply Obligation

The bill codified the National Domestic Gas Supply and Pricing Policy and Regulations 2008, which imposes supply obligations on gas producers based on the annual downstream demand requirement. The domestic market model supported by the bill was introduced by the government to ensure gas availability to the local economy pending when the local market can justify abundant supply of gas to wholesale customers[103]. Under the bill, the Upstream Petroleum Inspectorate (UPI) and DPRA are empowered to monitor and ensure that the gas suppliers meet their domestic gas supply obligations.[104] Some of the sanctions for not complying with the domestic gas supply obligations include payment of penalties; prevention of supplies for gas export for the period of non-compliance and where the period extends beyond 3 months, the relevant gas export license will be revoked.[105]

f. Gas Flaring and Environmental Standards

The PIB does not make provisions specifying clear and specific timelines for a total flare out date. Section 275 of the PIB provides that natural gas shall not be flared or vented after '*the flare-out date*' to be prescribed by the Minister. The Minister can, however, grant permit to gas producing companies to flare gas after the flare-out date. The grant of such permit shall be in the case of start-up, equipment failure, shut down, safety flaring or inability of customer

---

[103] Section 273(4) of the PIB provides that when the domestic and export markets attain parity, the gas market will be deregulated.
[104] Section 270 of the PIB
[105] Section 272 of the PIB

to off-take gas. The permit shall be for a period of not more than 100 days, or such longer period determined by the Minister.[106] There is no clear and specific timeline in the PIB for the total flare-out date. When the flare-out date is announced, the Minister shall also prescribe a new penalty regime for gas flared after the flare-out date. The fine shall not be less than the value of gas flared or vented.[107] Also, the certificates issued under section 3(2) of the Associated Gas Re-injection Act[108],(where the Minister is satisfied that the utilization or re-injection of produced gas is not appropriate or feasible) prior to the date the bill becomes law shall continue to have effect until they lapse.[109]

g. Fiscal provisions relating to gas undertakings

The PIB proposes a new tax called the Nigerian Hydrocarbon Tax to replace the Petroleum Profits Tax in the upstream sector.

Nigerian Hydrocarbon Tax (NHT) - The Bill introduces a new tax to be known as Nigerian Hydrocarbon Tax (NHT) to replace the Petroleum Profits Tax (PPT). The Nigerian Hydrocarbon Tax is to be levied upon the profits of any company engaged in upstream gas operations at the rate of 50% of the chargeable profit of a company engaged in on shore and shallow waters upstream operations, and 25% of the chargeable profit of a company engaged in upstream gas operations in deep water areas and frontier acreages.

Companies Income Tax (CIT) - The PIB makes the Companies Income Tax (as amended by the PIB) applicable to the upstream gas sector at the rate of 30% of the total profit of the gas company in its upstream operations. Companies involved in the downstream gas

---

[106] Section 277 of the PIB

[107] See section 281 of the PIB

[108] Section 3(2) of the Associated Gas Re-Injection Act provides that *'where the Minister is satisfied that utilization or re-injection of the produced gas is not appropriate or feasible in a particular field or fields, he may issue a certificate in that respect to a company engaged in the production of oil and gas, (a) specifying such terms and conditions, as he may at his discretion choose to impose, for the continued flaring of gas in the particular field or fields; (b) or permitting the company to continue to flare gas in the particular field or fields if the company pays such sum as the Minister may from time to time prescribe for every 28.317 Standard Cubic Metre (SCM) of gas flared'*

[109] Section 283 of the PIB

sector are already subject to Companies Income Tax at the rate of 30% under the Companies Income Tax Act. Any company involved in both upstream petroleum operations and downstream petroleum operations shall determine the companies income tax separately for its upstream petroleum operations and its downstream petroleum operations. In determining the Companies Income Tax payable, the NHT shall not be deductible.

Increased Tax Liability for gas producers - The implication of the application of NHT and CIT is far reaching for upstream gas undertakings. Companies producing gas in onshore and shallow water areas who currently pay only 30% Companies Income Tax will, in addition, be required to pay 50% Nigerian Hydrocarbon Tax. This implies that gas producers in onshore and shallow waters would be subject to a tax rate which is 50% higher than their current tax liability. Companies producing gas in deep water areas and frontier acreages who currently pay only 30% Companies Income Tax will, in addition, be required to pay 25% Nigerian Hydrocarbon Tax. This implies that gas producers in deep water areas and frontier acreages will be subject to a tax rate which is 25% higher than their current tax liability. Companies operating in the downstream petroleum sector will only pay the Companies Income Tax at the rate of 30%.

As mentioned earlier, increased tax liability for gas producing companies could adversely affect further investment in gas exploration and production. If this happens, the security of gas supply for Nigeria's rapidly expanding domestic gas market will be adversely affected. The security of supply for the export market will also be affected negatively as a result of difficulties that may arise in meeting new demands from new foreign customers.

Fiscal Incentives for Gas - Part VIII(9) of the bill makes only the initial 3 year tax holiday downstream gas incentives in section 39 of Companies Income Tax Act applicable to companies engaged in upstream gas operations on the condition that the gas supply destination is solely to the domestic market. Part VIII(7) of the PIB also amends Section 31(2)(a)(ii) of Companies Income Tax Act which provides for losses of previous years of assessment to be set-off against subsequent profits for the first 3 years of commencement of business to remove the limit of 3 years from commencement of business, by deleting the proviso in Companies Income Tax Act *'but such deductions shall not be made against the profit of the company after the fourth year from the year of commencement of such business'*. Therefore, there is no limit as to setting-off previous loss against future profits. This means that in future, companies can recover any amount of loss from future profits before such profits are subjected to tax.

CHAPTER FIVE

CHALLENGES TO ENERGY SECURITY IN NIGERIA's GAS SECTOR

This chapter discusses the various challenges that undermine Nigeria's aspirations to achieve energy security in gas. Issues such as gas flaring, inadequate gas infrastructure, gas pricing, political risks and global competition are considered in this chapter.

5.1   Gas flaring

Gas flaring is the process through which gas is burnt using an elevated vertical stack as the gas exits the flare stacks on oil wells or oil rigs. Gas flaring in Nigeria began since the inception of petroleum industry in the country[110]. Gas flaring became so rampant in Nigeria that it was regarded as a dominant feature of Nigeria's upstream activities[111]. The rate of gas flaring in Nigeria could make an uninformed individual to believe that natural gas, unlike crude oil, is not lucrative and at best can be treated as a by-product of oil. The Nigerian energy industry was therefore for a long period, replete with the practice of flaring gas with its ecological consequences and attendant waste of resources. Nigeria for a long time has remained one of the major gas flaring nations. However, in recent times, the flares are beginning to reduce.

a.   Why gas is flared in Nigeria

The oil producing companies initially cited the high cost of producing gas as a major reason for gas flaring in Nigeria. To put it succinctly, it was cheaper to flare gas than to utilize it. This was occasioned by the nature of the gas value chain, which is more complex than that of crude oil. Before gas is produced, there must be a buyer or end user available to take the gas. Fewer and more complex infrastructure and processes were required to transport the gas to the buyer or end user, unlike oil which was transported very easily. The absence of gas based industries and a ready domestic market to boost local demand for gas,[112] and the absence of adequate gas infrastructure also contributed to the continued flaring of gas. Despite the fiscal incentives such as tax holidays for gas utilization companies and

---

[110] Osuoka A. and Roderick P. 2005 Gas flaring in Nigeria: A Human Rights, Environmental and Economic Monstrosity. *A joint report written by the Environmental Rights Actions/ Friends of the Earth, Nigeria and the Climate Justice Programme; Amsterdam Press.*

[111] Okoh, R. N. 'Cost-Benefit analysis of Gas production in Nigeria: Nigerian Economic Society (NES), Natural Resource Use, The Environment and Sustainable Development, Ibadan: NES August 20, 2013, cited in Aghalino, S.O, 'Gas flaring, environmental pollution and abatement measures in Nigeria- 1969-2001' Vol. 11, No4 Journal of Sustainable development in Africa 2009

[112] African Development Consulting Group (ADCG) The Nigerian Gas Industry: A Survey 1996.

regulations prohibiting gas flaring, Nigeria is yet to achieve zero gas flaring rate. This outcome could be as a result of a dysfunctional incentive system and investment climate. The World Bank's GGFR Partnership programme[113] shows that effective enforcement of regulations and the provision of the right incentives are crucial to reducing gas flaring. Sadly most developing countries lack efficient and effective regulations on gas flaring[114]. GGFR targets of 30 per cent reduction in global gas flaring by end of 2017.

b. Gas flaring indices

Nigeria produced an estimated 285306.95 million tons of natural gas between 1961 and 1998.[115] Nigeria flared an estimated 234021.19 million tons of natural gas produced within the period, representing 82.69% of all the gas produced in the same period. Nigeria flared 99% of the gas produced in 1970.[116] Nigeria produced an estimated 30,947.657 Bcf of natural gas between 1997 and 2013.[117] Nigeria flared an estimated 12,455.263 Bcf of natural gas produced within the period, representing 40.2% of all the gas produced in the same period.[118]

---

[113] This programme provides for a platform whereby, governments, companies and other key stakeholders come together and take collaborative measures, facilitate gas projects, as well as curb the barriers associated with gas utilization. The World Bank's Global Gas Flaring Reduction (GGFR) Partnership programme is a public-private partnership which was launched at the World Summit on Sustainable Development in Johannesburg in 2002. The initiative was put in place by the World Bank to achieve zero global gas flaring.

[114] The World Bank, 'Regulation of Associated Gas Flaring and Venting: A Global Overview and Lessons from International Experience' Global gas flaring reduction- a public-private partnership: No. 3, Washington, DC

[115] Aghalino S.O. 'Gas flaring, environmental pollution and abatement measures in Nigeria' - 1969-2001 Vol. 11, No. 4 Journal of Sustainable development in Africa 2009

[116] ibid

[117] Figures sourced and deduced from NNPC Annual Statistical Bulletins from 1997 to 2013, by Elo Adhekpukoli, in April 2015

[118] ibid

Year	Estimated Gas Produced (Bcf)	Estimated Gas Flared (Bcf)	% of gas flared
1997	1,142	801.8	70.2%
1998	1,308	834.5	63.79%
1999	1,328	798.42	60.12%
2000	1,599	882.760	55.20%
2001	1,823	920.760	50.51%
2002	1,652	744.108	45.04%
2003	1,828.542	846.014	46.26%
2004	2,082.283	885.761	42.53%
2005	2,093.629	812.333	38.80%
2006	2,182.43	799.99	36.65%
2007	2,415.65	789.55	32.68%
2008	2,282.44	631.19	27.65%
2009	1,837.278	509.351	27.72%
2010	2,392.838	581.568	24.30%
2011	2,400.402	619.032	25.78%
2012	2,580.165	588.666	22.81%
2013	2,325.14	409.31	18%

Nigeria has gradually moved from flaring 100% of its gas in 1958 to less than 20% in 2013. This development is commendable. Nigeria is however still the second highest gas flaring nation in the world. Available World Bank statistics show that by the end of 2011, 10 countries accounted for 74% of the total gas flared globally. [119] The top ten leading contributors to world gas flaring at the end of 2011, were (in declining order) Russia, Nigeria, Iran, Iraq, USA, Algeria, Kazakhstan, Angola, Saudi Arabia and Venezuela.

---

[119] World Bank, 'Estimated Flared Volumes from Satellite Data, 2007-2011'. World Bank 'Estimated Flared Volumes from Satellite Data, 2007-2011' http://web.worldbank.org/WBSITE/EXTERNAL/TOPICS/EXTOGMC/EXT GGFR/0,,contentMDK:22137498-pagePK:64168445-piPK:64168309- theSitePK:5780 last accessed on 10th April, 2015

Country	% share of global gas flared by end of 2011
Russia	27%
Nigeria	11%
Iran	8%
Iraq	7%
USA	5%
Algeria	4%
Kazakhstan	3%
Angola	3%
Saudi Arabia	3%
Venezuela	3%

Satellite data obtained by the National Geophysical Data Centre[120] shows that from 2005 to 2010, global gas flaring decreased by about 20%. Russia and Nigeria made the most significant reductions in terms of volume of gas flared.

c. Negative impact of gas flaring in Nigeria

Nigeria became a major contributor to global ecological crisis as a result of gas flaring. Osuaka and Roderick[121] posit that the burning of fossil fuel, coal, oil and greenhouse gases has been inducing global warming and this may get worse during the 21st century. The gas flared exhausts the stratospheric layer of the atmosphere which protects the earth from ultra violet radiation. Gas flaring has also been identified as a major cause of acidic rain in gas producing areas. Flared gas produces sulphur which mixes with atmospheric compounds such as water and oxygen. According to the Commonwealth, *"Mankind is the ultimate loser in this assault against mother nature."* [122] Gas flaring in Nigeria, can be likened to an impoverished

---

[120] World Bank 'Global Gas Flaring Reduction Partnership (GGFR),' October 2011 Brochure; see also Christopher Elvidge et al Estimation of Gas Flaring Volumes Using NASA MODIS Fire Detection Products' NOAA's National Geophysical Data Center (NGDC) annual report, February 8, 2011.

[121] Supra, see note 73

[122] Holgate Martin, 'Climate Change: Meeting the Challenges'. Report by Commonwealth group of Experts, London: Commonwealth Secretariat 1989, cited in Aghalino S.O. 'Gas flaring, environmental pollution and abatement measures in

mien heaving the bulk of his sweated earnings into a flowing stream. So much is needed yet much more is lost. The colossal economic loss as a result of gas flaring can best be imagined.

As discussed earlier in chapters two and three, the efforts made by the Nigerian government and industry operators to reduce gas flaring and utilize gas in Nigeria. Notably, initial efforts towards ending gas flaring were private sector driven as from 1963, when oil producing companies like Shell began to supply gas to industries. Such efforts were however very minimal and the dearth of investments in gas utilization exposed the reluctance of the oil producing companies to stop gas flaring. The Nigerian government soon woke up in the 1970s to the reality that the abundant gas resources could be utilized to transform the economy of the country. It was after this awakening that the government began to develop a policy focus geared towards gas utilization.

5.2 Inadequate Gas Infrastructure

The nature of gas as a commodity makes the development of infrastructure for supply and storage of the commodity imperative. Unfortunately, Nigeria has a lot to do in this regard.

a. Pipeline infrastructure

Domestic gas transportation through pipelines is more economically efficient and safer than the use of trucks. Before the NGC was established in 1988, inadequate pipeline network for gas transportation was a major factor that adversely affected gas utilization in Nigeria. Most companies requiring gas were unfortunately isolated from gas supply due to the inadequate pipeline infrastructure in the country. The various LPG depots scattered all over the country are also affected by the inadequate pipeline infrastructure. Most of the inland LPG depots are isolated from gas supply, which accounts partly for the low utilization of LPG in Nigeria. The utilization of gas for power generation has also suffered much due to inadequate pipeline infrastructure connecting the power plants to the gas fields. As was explained earlier in Chapter Three, most of the power plants built by Nigeria's former President, Olusegun Obasanjo, between 2000 and 2007, could not commence power generation upon completion because there were no pipelines to supply the gas required to generate electricity.

b. Storage infrastructure

As mentioned earlier in Chapter Two the Nigerian government constructed nine LPG depots located at Apapa, Calabar, Enugu, Makurdi, Ibadan, Ilorin, Kano, Gombe and Gusau. The depots were constructed to boost gas storage facilities around the country to promote the utilization of LPG. The intention of the government that the inland depots will aid the widespread utilization of LPG is still far from being achieved. Considering the geographical spread of Nigeria, each state capital ought to have LPG depots for greater accessibility by consumers. Unfortunately, there have been no further developments of LPG storage depots and most of the existing depots are not functional.

5.3   Gas Pricing

Gas pricing in Nigeria's domestic market is still uncompetitive and yet to be market driven. The current practice of setting end user prices in the Nigerian domestic gas market at levels below international gas prices is counter-productive. These low prices have provided limited commercial incentive for investors to develop and produce Nigeria's gas resources for the domestic market.

a. Disparity in domestic and export gas prices

Prior to 2015, the disparity in the domestic and export gas prices was much. Before the increase of gas price to the power sector to $2.50 US dollars per mcf and $0.80 cents per mcf for transportation costs[123]

---

[123] The Presidential Task Force on Power, 'Gas Price Increase Will Boost Electricity   Supply' http://nigeriapowerreform.org/index.php?option=com_content&view=article&id =1730:gas-price-increase-will-boost-electricity-supply-says-nerc&catid=36:sector-news&Itemid=336 last accessed on 8th April, 2015

in 2015, domestic gas price to the power sector was below $2.00 US dollars per mcf until 2014. However, natural gas prices in the international market averaged $3.93US dollars per mcf from 1990 until 2015, reaching an all time high of $15.39 US dollars per mcf in December 2005.[124] The current average price for natural gas as at April, 2015, is $2.67 US dollars per mcf.[125] Industry players in Nigeria therefore focused more on gas exports to the detriment of gas supply to the domestic market. This was one of the reasons the Domestic Gas Supply Obligation was introduced to compel gas producers to reserve some percentage of their gas production for the domestic market. It is hoped that as domestic gas prices become commercially driven, Nigeria will be better positioned for security of gas supply to the domestic gas market.

5.4   Political risks

During the period of militancy in the Niger Delta where the bulk of Nigeria's gas deposits and investments are located, oil and gas production fell to below 50% of the expected daily output. This occurred progressively between 2003 and 2007 before the amnesty programme for the militants was introduced.[126] This fall in production resulted from forced shut down of facilities, evacuation of key staff and vandalization of oil and gas installations by militants and restive youths. While militancy has largely abated after the amnesty programme was introduced, community youth restiveness and vandalisation of oil and gas installations have continued. The constant vandalisation of gas pipelines supplying gas to power generation plants for example, have continued to be a setback for the power sector reforms. Operators could be unwilling to invest huge funds in gas infrastructure if they are not sure of security for such assets. The gas sector, therefore suffers the effect of such paucity of

---

[124] Trading Economics, http://www.tradingeconomics.com/commodity/natural-gas last accessed on 8th April, 2015
[125] ibid
[126] Olasupo Olusola, *The Consequences of Militancy in Nigeria's Niger Delta'* 2013, Transcampus Journal of Research in National Development (JORIND). See also Fidelis E. Arong & Agbere M Ikechuckwu *'The Effect of the Cost of Militancy and Unrest or Peace Accounting on the Productivity of Private Organisations in Nigeria'* 2013, International Journal of Public Administration and Management Research (IJPAMR), Vol. 2, No.1 2013

investments, which is inimical to achieving energy security.

5.5   Global competition

a. US Shale gas

Shale gas is classified as unconventional natural gas. Unconventional natural gas refers to natural gas that is more difficult and less economical to extract mainly because of specialized technology required to access and exploit it.[127]   Shale gas is extracted directly from fossil shale rocks, which have low permeability. The gas resource is difficult to obtain as a result of the low permeability of shale rocks. The main technology used to exploit shale gas is hydraulic fracturing (fracking). Fracking is a technique by which the shale rocks are shattered underground. Water, sand and chemicals are pumped into the shale rocks to create cracks through which gas escapes to the surface. The fracking technique was developed by George Mitchell[128] who spent about 10 years researching how shale gas can be extracted. The extraction of shale gas through fracking is being challenged because of concerns that the fracking method will pollute underground water[129].

Shale gas now contributes a third of America's gas supplies.[130] A few years ago, the United States in her quest for security in energy supplies embarked on development of shale oil and gas. The US has now overtaken Russia as the world's largest gas producer as a result of shale gas. According to Jean Abiteboul,[131] Cheniere's head of marketing, 'we underestimated the magnitude of shale gas'.

---

[127] Judith Kim and Rebecca Downes, *Unconventional Gas: Time to take the "Un" out of Unconventional?* International Comparative Legal Guide to: *Gas Regulation 2012*, Global Law Group, 2012.

[128] The Economist, 'America's Bounty: Gas Works' 14th July, 2012

[129] Sean Sweeney and Lara Skinner, 'Global Shale Gas and the Anti-Fracking Movement: Developing Union Perspectives and Approaches' Working Paper No. 1, published by Trade Unions for Energy Democracy, in cooperation with the Rosa Luxemburg Stiftung – New York Office and the Global Labor Institute at Cornell University, June 2014.

[130] ibid

[131] Cited in Guy Chazan 'Shale Gas: Terminal decline no longer' The Financial Times 23rd April, 2012 http://www.ft.com/intl/cms/s/0/a5053c50-8d2b-11e1-9798-00144feab49a.html last accessed on 10th April, 2015

However, the impact of shale gas developments in the United States is far reaching for Nigeria's energy security in the gas export market. The NLNG once exported 10% of its annual capacity to the United States through the Lake Charles Terminal. Today, that market is closed.[132] United States is now converting its LNG import terminals to export terminals. In 2003, Cheniere Energy in the United States built a LNG import terminal at Sabine Pass, USA, in 2012, the company invested $10billion US dollars to convert it into an LNG export terminal. Cheniere is one of the many companies that plan to export surplus US gas at cheaper prices. According to Chariff Souki[133] the United States plans to introduce the freedom of the North American gas market to other countries. Cheniere and other US companies not only intend to sell at lower prices indexed to Henry Hub price rather than being indexed to oil, they intend to do away with the take or pay clause, giving consumers the liberty to take more or less gas than they contracted for. This would revolutionize the international gas market where traditionally, gas sales contracts are tied up for as much as 20 years on take or pay basis and prices are indexed to oil prices. Contracting the sale of gas on a take or pay basis meant that buyers agreed to pay penalty if they took less than the volume of gas they contracted for. Gas suppliers preferred such rigid arrangements because of the certainty they need to invest in gas production, which is capital intensive and complex.

This move by the US companies could force other gas exporters to reduce their prices and review their contracts to keep their customers. Developments like this would affect Nigeria's revenue projections from gas exports. The possibility of losing some market share in the international gas market due to shale gas development in the United States is a threat to Nigeria's energy security in the international gas market.

---

[132] Victor Eromosele, 'US Shale Gas Revolution & Global Impact' Paper presented at the Centre for Petroleum Institute, Petroleum Policy Roundtable (PPRXII), Golden Gate Restaurant, Lagos, 20th July, 2012

[133] Guy Chazan, 'Shale Gas: Terminal Decline no longer' Financial Times 23rd April, 2012 http://www.ft.com/intl/cms/s/0/a5053c50-8d2b-11e1-9798-00144feab49a.html last accessed on 10th April, 2015

b. New gas discoveries in the eastern coast of Africa

Angola, Mozambique and Tanzania are set to join the African LNG exporters by 2020. New gas discoveries in the last 3 years has seen Mozambique's reserves updated from 4 Tcf of gas to about 100 Tcf of proven natural gas reserves, placing the country as the third-largest proven natural gas reserve holder in Africa, after Nigeria and Algeria[134]. Mozambique currently supplies much of its produced gas to South Africa via the 535-mile Sasol Petroleum International Gas Pipeline. The US-based Anadarko and Italy-based Eni have agreed to develop two onshore 5-million-tons-per-annum (Mmtpa) (or 240 Bcf) liquefied natural gas (LNG) trains. Anadarko has signed non-binding long-term supply agreements with Asian buyers covering two-thirds of the capacity of the first 5-Mmtpa liquefaction train. First LNG sales are expected in 2019.[135]

Tanzania has an estimated 46.5 Tcf of natural gas reserves.[136] In 2008, Tanzania upgraded its 2008 production sharing agreement for gas and opened tenders for seven deepwater blocks and one block on Lake Tanganyika. The 2013 model Tanzania Production Sharing Agreement template retained many provisions from the 2008 model, including minimum state participation of 25 percent, additional profits tax, and government royalty, but it also encouraged deepwater exploration by reducing the royalty rate to 7.5 percent from 12.5 percent.[137] The BG Group, in partnership with Ophir Energy, and Statoil, in partnership with ExxonMobil, have made several offshore natural gas discoveries in Tanzania since 2010, totaling 25 to 30 Tcf of recoverable gas resources. The Tanzanian government, Statoil, ExxonMobil, BG Group, and Ophir Energy are currently working on plans to develop a joint LNG plant.[138]

---

[134] U.S. Energy Information Administration, 'Independent Statistics & Analysis, Mozambique Country Analysis Note' last updated July 2014 http://www.eia.gov/countries/country-data.cfm?fips=mz last accessed April 11, 2015.

[135] ibid

[136] John Daly, 'Fast Growing Tanzania Looks to Begin LNG Production By 2020' The Oil Price, 30th April 2014. http://oilprice.com/Energy/Natural-Gas/Fast-Growing-Tanzania-Looks-To-Begin-LNG-Production-By-2020.html last accessed on 10th April, 2015

[137] ibid

[138] U.S. Energy Information Administration, 'Independent Statistics & Analysis,

The Tanzanian government intends to encourage gas exploration and believes that Tanzania can achieve gas discoveries of up to 200 Tcf that would make Tanzania become the country with the largest proven gas reserves in Africa, overtaking Nigeria. Tanzania plans to export its first LNG by 2020 and is in a hot race with Mozambique to become East Africa's first LNG exporter.

The new discoveries and developments in Mozambique and Tanzania have the potential to affect Nigeria's market share in world LNG trade and affect Nigeria's energy security in the international gas market. Mozambique and Tanzania are located on the eastern African coast separated from the rest of Asia by the Indian Ocean. This location strategically positions them to compete for the Asian and Far-East Asian major gas consumers like India, Japan and China. Angola will also compete for the American and European gas markets with Nigeria on the Atlantic Basin. The entrance of Angola, Mozambique and Tanzania, adds to the competition from Algeria for the European gas market and competition from Russia and Central Asian countries like Qatar and Kazakhstan for gas markets in Japan and China.

Tanzania Country Analysis Note' Last updated in April 2014 http://www.eia.gov/countries/country-data.cfm?fips=tz last accessed April 11, 2015

CHAPTER SIX

HOW NIGERIA CAN ACHIEVE ENERGY SECURITY IN GAS

This concluding chapter discusses how Nigeria can reposition herself to overcome her challenges and make use of opportunities to achieve energy security in gas, taking into consideration, the need to balance security of supply in the domestic market and security of demand in the export market.

Energy security is essential in the 21st Century, and there cannot be any pretense about it. It is safe to agree with Yergin's view that today, the concept of energy security needs to be expanded to include the protection of the entire energy supply chain and infrastructure.[139] In a world of increasing interdependence, energy security will depend much on how countries manage their relations with one another, whether bilaterally or within multilateral frameworks. The investment climate itself must become a key concern in energy security. There needs to be a continual flow of investment and technology in order for new resources to be developed. These capital flows will not materialize without reasonable and stable investment frameworks, timely decision-making by governments, open markets and guaranteed security for critical infrastructure.[140] Energy security can only be achieved through adequate investments that are coherent and consistent.

A robust and secure energy base requires a strategic and deliberate government policy, both short and long term, to guarantee the present and future energy needs of the country. Nigeria cannot survive for long on policy documents, which can easily be jettisoned by new government regimes. Such government policy must be complemented by stable and progressive legal framework. If Nigeria is to achieve her aspirations for development, Nigeria must put in place adequate measures towards energy security in her gas sector. Such measures would include, amongst other things, having in place a comprehensive legal framework for gas, as soon as possible to drive business decisions by gas investors.

The draft Petroleum Industry Bill has undergone several reviews for over a decade and the current 2012 version is still pending before the National Assembly. During this prolonged delay in enacting the Bill into law, investments have gone to other African countries like Angola, Tanzania and Mozambique. The current fiscal regime for gas undertakings in the 2012 version of the draft bill also has the potential of scaring investments away from gas exploration and development in Nigeria due to increased fiscal obligations for

---

[139] Supra, see note 12
[140] Ibid

operators compared to what currently obtains in the sector. Enacting the current version of the Bill without amendments to effect some significant reduction in the fiscal obligations for gas undertakings could be counter-productive. After so much uncertainty spanning over a decade regarding the bill, it is not likely that an amendment would be easy to come by once it is enacted into law. The Bill has the potential of determining the future of gas in Nigeria but it is important to get the fiscal provisions right.

Aside from the fiscal provisions, the provisions on gas pricing, domestic supply, anti-trust, consumer protection and licensing are great and have the potential to revolutionize the domestic gas market. Although some minor amendments to the anti-trust and market regulations provisions of the bill as it affects the downstream gas sector will be necessary to define dominance thresholds, expressly prohibit market dominance, and set a specific time for the issuance of consumer protection regulations.

Borok, Agandu and Morgan[141], have identified corruption as one of the major challenges affecting Nigeria's energy sector and this has to be tackled if the country is to make any head way in energy security. The National Extractive Industries Transparency Initiative (NEITI) has brought significant transparency in terms of accurate declaration of gas discoveries, production and revenue. Transparency in data reporting is important for the effective and judicious utilization of government revenue derived from gas development. Nigeria should also use her energy wealth to maximize linkages from the extractive sector to the rest of the economy through development of infrastructure and human capital that will stimulate broad-based development in other sectors of the economy such as the agriculture, manufacturing and processing industries. This would lead to more job creation for the young and teeming population. The failure to do so can undermine long-term energy security, primarily by causing social tensions and restiveness.[142] The experience with militancy, youth restiveness and vandalization of critical oil and gas infrastructure by disgruntled youths is an eye opener for Nigeria.

[141] Supra, see note 2
[142] Jorrit Rients Oppewal, 'Energy Security in Nigeria' ISPI Analysis, No. 86, December 2011

Urgent and continuous steps must be taken to ensure that Nigeria does not go that way again.

Instability in Algeria and Libya, and Russia's continuous aggression against Ukraine makes Nigeria a viable alternative gas supplier to the European Union. Although the Caspian region may hold great potential for new natural gas supplies for Europe, supplies have to transit Russia to arrive in the European market. The Caspian region therefore does not pose much threat to Nigeria's potential as an alternative gas supplier to the European Union. While the feasibility of the trans-Saharan gas pipeline originally designed to supply Nigerian gas to Europe, is in doubt due to increased insecurity and instability in Northern Nigeria and North African countries due to terrorist activities of Boko Haram and other terrorist groups, Nigeria can position herself through increased LNG capacity. The completion of the Olokola LNG and the Brass LNG projects therefore becomes an immediate necessity.

Nigeria's immediate competitor for the European gas market, interestingly, is the United States due to the development of shale gas that has now made the United States the world's largest gas producer. For many parts of Europe, especially the Baltic region and Central Europe, where the United States enjoys strong and friendly relations, any decision to export US LNG to that region would be welcomed as a potential offset to their dependence on Russian gas. However, the bigger effect of US entry into global LNG sales may be on pricing rather than supplies. With new investments in gas exploration and development, Nigeria will be in a better position to compete with emerging competitors in the global gas market such as the United States, Mozambique and Tanzania.

Nigeria can also strengthen her regional position as the major gas supplier to ECOWAS Countries. West Africa can depend on Nigeria the way the European Union depends largely on Russia for gas supply. This can be achieved by maximizing the West African Gas Pipeline, which was developed to supply gas to Benin Republic, Togo and Ghana in particular. There is also the potential of extending the pipeline to other West African countries, especially taking into consideration the fact that most of the commercial nerve centres of

West African countries are located along the coast from Lagos to Dakar.

Unfortunately, Nigeria has been unable to meet her supply obligations to the three countries currently connected to the West African Gas Pipeline, especially Ghana, which is the biggest gas consumer amongst the three countries. Ghana has complained about shortage of supply and is already making long-term plans to reduce her dependence on Nigeria for gas.[143] If Ghana is able to develop gas fields or purchase gas from other gas producing nations other than Nigeria, the purpose of constructing the West African Gas Pipeline will be defeated. It is important for Nigeria to strengthen her position as a dependable gas supplier in the West African sub-region. If Nigeria loses her market share in the export gas market in West Africa, Nigeria's revenue generation drive from gas export would be adversely impacted.

Another important measure Nigeria must take is to address the issue of security of gas facilities and installations to check vandalism and sabotage. Nigeria will also need to address the social issues that have led to the proliferation of militancy and youth restiveness especially in the Niger Delta region. While the amnesty programme has achieved some significant results in this regard, it remains to be seen how the new government regime led by President Muhammadu Buhari will handle the situation in the Niger Delta.

Finally, Nigeria should be primarily concerned with balancing both security of foreign demand for Nigerian gas to earn foreign exchange and security of supply of gas to the domestic market to drive economic development. Nigeria cannot afford to forego one for the other for now.

---

[143] Johnson Alabi, 'Ghana Set to Cut Gas Supply from Nigeria' Energy News January 8, 2015. http://energynews-ng.com/ghana-set-to-cut-gas-supply-from-nigeria/ last accessed on 9th April, 2015

REFERENCES

Abayomi Awobokun, *'Developing the Domestic LPG Market: Challenges and Prospects,'* A presentation made at the Centre for Petroleum Information (CPI) 12th Petroleum Policy Round Table, July 20, 2012

Abdallah S. Jum'ah *'A Perspective on Energy Security'* in 'The New Energy Security Paradigm' 2006 African Development Consulting Group, 'The Nigerian Gas Industry: A Survey' 1996

Aghalino, S.O, *'Gas flaring, environmental pollution and abatement measures in Nigeria- 1969-2001'* Vol. 11, No4 Journal of Sustainable development in Africa 2009

Argus Media Limited, *Statistical Review of Global LP Gas, 2013*

Austin Avuru, *'Strategies for Sustaining Gas to Power Agenda for Economic and Industrial Growth: The Upstream Point of View: What incentive to invest when demand is unsure?'* published in Nigerian Gas Journal of the Nigerian Gas Association, 'Insights into Nigeria's Gas Revolution' Half Year Edition 2013

Chidi Orazulike, *'Energy Crisis: The Bane of Nigeria's Development,'* Oilgas Magazine, December 12, 2013, cited in Maren Borok et al 'Energy Security in Nigeria: Challenges and Way Forward' International Journal of Engineering Science Innovation, Volume 2 Issue 11, November, 2013

Christopher Elvidge et al, *'NOAA's National Geophysical Data Center Annual Report'*, February 8, 2011

Daniel Fiott, Patrice Yamba T. Kantu and Florian Peter Iwinjak, *'Energy Security'* published in 'Climate Change and Security in Africa' Vulnerability Discussion Paper

Daniel Yergin, *'Ensuring Energy Security'* Council of Foreign Relations 2006

David Ige, *'Gas Revolution Agenda: Status Update'*, published in Nigerian Gas Journal of the Nigerian Gas Association, 'Insights into Nigeria's Gas Revolution' Half Year Edition 2013

Edward Davey, Secretary of State for Energy and Climate Change *'Energy Security Strategy'* Department of Energy and Climate Change, November 2012, presented to Parliament by the Secretary of State for Energy and Climate Change by Command of Her Majesty

Florian Baumann *'Energy Security as multidimensional concept'* Research Group on European Affairs, Centre for Applied Policy Research, March 2008

Fidelis E. Arong & Agbere M Ikechuckwu *'The Effect of the Cost of Militancy and Unrest or Peace Accounting on the Productivity of Private Organisations in Nigeria'* 2013, International Journal of Public Administration and Management Research (IJPAMR), Vol. 2, No.1 2013

Funsho Kupolokun, *'Nigeria and the future gas market'*, a lecture delivered by the then Group Managing Director of the Nigerian National Petroleum Corporation at the Baker Institute Energy Forum, Rice University, 2006

International Finance Corporation *'Environmental, Health, and Safety Guidelines for onshore oil and gas development'* 2007

Jorrit Rients Oppewal, *'Energy Security in Nigeria'* ISPI Analysis, No. 86, December 2011

Judith Kim and Rebecca Downes, *'Unconventional Gas: Time to take the "Un" out of Unconventional?'* International Comparative Legal Guide to: Gas Regulation 2012, Global Law Group, 2012

Maren Borok, Agontu Agandu and Mangai Morgan, *'Energy Security in Nigeria: Challenges and Way Forward'* International Journal of

Engineering Science Innovation, Volume 2 Issue 11, November, 2013

Matthew H. Brown, Christie Rewey and Troy Gagliano *'Energy Security'* National Conference of State Legislatures, April 2003

Michael Ratner, Paul Belkin, Jim Nichol, Steven Woehrel, *'Europe's Energy Security: Options and Challenges to Natural Gas Supply Diversification'* Congressional Research Service Report for Congress, August 20, 2013

Nigeria Liquefied Natural Gas Limited *'Facts & Figures on NLNG 2014'*

Nigeria Gas Master Plan, 2008

NNPC Annual Statistical Bulletins from 1997 to 2013

Okoh, R. N. *'Cost-Benefit analysis of Gas production in Nigeria'*: Nigerian Economic Society (NES), Natural Resource Use, The Environment and Sustainable Development, Ibadan: NES August 20, 2013, cited in Aghalino, S.O, 'Gas flaring, environmental pollution and abatement measures in Nigeria-1969-2001' Vol. 11, No4 Journal of Sustainable development in Africa 2009

Olasupo Olusola, *'The Consequences of Militancy in Nigeria's Niger Delta'* 2013, Transcampus Journal of Research in National Development (JORIND)

Osuoka A. and Roderick P. *'Gas flaring in Nigeria: A Human Rights, Environmental and Economic Monstrosity.'* A joint report written by the Environmental Rights Actions/ Friends of the Earth, Nigeria and the Climate Justice Programme; Amsterdam Press, 2005

Sean Sweeney and Lara Skinner, *'Global Shale Gas and the Anti-Fracking Movement: Developing Union Perspectives and Approaches'* Working Paper No. 1, published by Trade Unions for Energy

Democracy, in cooperation with the Rosa Luxemburg Stiftung – New York Office and the Global Labor Institute at Cornell University, June 2014.

The Presidency, Federal Republic of Nigeria, Energy Commission *National Energy Policy'* 2003

The Economist, *'America's Bounty: Gas Works'* 14th July, 2012

Ukpohor Excel *'Nigerian Gas Master Plan: Strengthening The Nigeria Gas Infrastructure Blueprint As A Base For Expanding Regional Gas Market,'* a technical paper delivered at the World Gas Conference 2009

Victor Eromosele, *'US Shale Gas Revolution & its Global Impact'* Paper presented at the Centre for Petroleum Institute, Petroleum Policy Roundtable (PPRXII), Golden Gate Restaurant, Lagos, 20th July, 2012

William J. Nuttall and Devon L. Manz,'A *'New Energy Security Paradigm for the Twenty-First Century'* Judge Business School, University of Cambridge

World Economic Forum in partnership with Cambridge Energy Research Associates, *'The New Energy Security Paradigm'* 2006

World Bank, *'Regulation of Associated Gas Flaring and Venting: A Global Overview and Lessons from International Experience'* Global gas flaring reduction- a public-private partnership: No. 3, Washington, DC

World Bank, *'The Nigerian LP Gas Sector Improvement Study'* Energy Sector Management Assistance Programme (ESMAP) Report, March 2004

World Bank, *'Global Gas Flaring Reduction Partnership (GGFR) Brochure, Estimation of Gas Flaring Volumes Using NASA MODIS Fire Detection Products'* October 2011

World LP Gas Association Annual Report 2013

Internet Sources
Euan Mearns *'Global Energy Trends – BP Statistical Review 2014'* Energy
Matters, June 17, 2014 www.euanmearns.com/global-energy-
trends-bp-statistical-review-2014/ last visited on 10th April,
2015

Guy Chazan *'Shale Gas: Terminal decline no longer'* The Financial Times,
23rd April, 2012 http://www.ft.com/intl/cms/s/0/a5053c50-
8d2b-11e1-9798-00144feab49a.html last accessed on 10th
April, 2015

International Energy Agency, *'Energy Security'*
http://www.iea.org/topics/energysecurity last accessed on
February 9, 2015

International Energy Agency *'Natural Gas'*,
www.iea.org/topics/naturalgas/ last accessed on February 10,
2015

Iowa State University, *'Liquid Fuel Measurements and Conversions'*
October 2008.
https://www.extension.iastate.edu/agdm/wholefarm/pdf/c6
-87.pdf last accessed 8th April, 2015

John Daly, *'Fast Growing Tanzania Looks to Begin LNG Production By
2020'* The Oil Price, 30th April 2014.
http://oilprice.com/Energy/Natural-Gas/Fast-Growing-
Tanzania-Looks-To-Begin-LNG-Production-By-2020.html
last accessed on 10th April, 2015

Johnson Alabi, *'Ghana Set to Cut Gas Supply from Nigeria'* Energy News
January 8, 2015. http://energynews-ng.com/ghana-set-to-
cut-gas-supply-from-nigeria/ last accessed on 9th April, 2015

NNPC Articles, *'Nigeria to Support EU Long Term Gas Supply Security'*
www.nnpcgroup.com/PublicRelations/NNPCinthenews/tabi
d/92/articleType/ArticleView/articleId/537/Nigeria-to-

Support-EU-Long-Term-Gas-Supply-Security.aspx. last accessed on 8th April, 2015

Okonjo Iweala, *Transforming the Nigerian Economy: Opportunities and Challenges'* 2014 Convocation Address delivered by the Co-ordinating Minister for the Economy and Hon. Minister of Finance at Babcock University, June, 2014. http://www.fmf.gov.ng/departments/economic-research-and-policy-management/190-transforming-the-nigerian-economy-opportunities-and-challenges.html last accessed on 8th April, 2015

Suma Chakrabarti, speech delivered at the GGFR Partnership Forum, London, 24th October 2012. http://www.ebrd.com/news/2012/speech-transcript-suma-chakrabarti-at-the-global-gas-flaring-reduction-ggfr-partnership-forum-on-24-october-2012-in-london-.html last accessed April 11, 2015

Trading Economics http://www.tradingeconomics.com/commodity/crude-oil last accessed on 8th April, 2015

Trading Economics, http://www.tradingeconomics.com/commodity/natural-gas last accessed on 8th April, 2015

UNFCCChttp://unfccc.int/essential_background/convention/status_of_ratification/items/2631.php last accessed October 27, 2014

U.S. Energy Information Administration, 'Independent Statistics & Analysis, Mozambique Country Analysis Note' last updated July 2014 http://www.eia.gov/countries/country-data.cfm?fips=mz last accessed April 11, 2015

U.S. Energy Information Administration, 'Independent Statistics & Analysis, Tanzania Country Analysis Note' Last updated in April 2014 http://www.eia.gov/countries/country-data.cfm?fips=tz last accessed April 11, 2015

World Bank *'Estimated Flared Volumes from Satellite Data, 2007-2011'*
http://web.worldbank.org/WBSITE/EXTERNAL/TOPIC
S/EXTOGMC/EXTGGFR/0,,contentMDK:22137498-
pagePK:64168445-piPK:64168309-theSitePK:5780 last
accessed on 10th April, 2015

World Bank, 'World Bank to help Nigeria Improve Gas Supply and
Bring More Electricity to Nigerian Consumers' Press Release,
April 2013 http://www.worldbank.org/en/news/press-
release/2013/04/22/world-bank-to-help-nigeria-improve-
gas-supply-and-reliability-and-bring-more-electricity-to-
nigerian-consumers last accessed 8th April, 2015